'Kindfulness is a simple idea that can change everything.'

Seth Godin

'This book is a wonderful antidote to the Donald Trump S̶
business with people if I don't feel I have to count my finge̶

Nick Jenkins, Fou̶n̶d̶e̶r̶ ̶o̶f̶ ̶M̶o̶o̶n̶p̶i̶g̶,̶ ̶B̶B̶C̶ ̶D̶r̶a̶g̶o̶n̶ ̶

'Kindness has been central to our approach to business at Timpson for many years. It's not fluffy or weak – it's strong, it builds great teams, and it leads to long-lasting success. Graham's brilliant book will show you how.'

James Timpson, CEO of Timpson

'This book puts kindness at the centre of social action. Kindness informs us and engages us in the well-being of others. Here's to us all moving forward to more kindness, and this book is definitely a good omen.'

Lord John Bird MBE, Founder of the Big Issue

'*KIND* is the business book I have always wanted to read. The insightful Graham Allcott has brought the power of kindness to us all, as his vulnerability, courage and wisdom shine through this book. One of the kindest and most powerful voices in the business world.'

Denise Nurse, CEO of Success Coach, Co-Founder of Black Founders Hub and BBC TV Presenter

'This book is your guide to maximizing others' potential without being a jerk. Swap scare tactics for psychological safety and become the charismatic, high-energy leader everyone loves working with.'

Jodie Cook, Founder of Coachvox and Senior Contributor, Forbes

'*KIND* is a keeper. With wit, warmth and wisdom, Allcott shows us how to harness the power of kindness to become better people, leading better lives in a better world. Grab a copy now!'

Carl Honoré, author of In Praise of Slow

'This book feels like a breath of fresh air. Rather than suggesting I strive to be something "more" in order to be successful in life and work, it reminds me to tap into something that's been right there all along. This book gives me permission to lean on my kindness, which is free, generates excellent outcomes, and fundamentally just feels good to use. A really powerful and useful read.'

Hannah Massarella, Founder of Bird

'I've always lived by the mantra "work hard, play hard, be kind" and it's excellent to now have this thoughtful, helpful guide to the why, what and how on what role kindness can have in the workplace. Another inspiring read from Graham that looks set to become an instant classic for any thoughtful leader's bookshelf.'

Sophie Devonshire, CEO of The Marketing Society & author, Superfast

'What a lovely book. Chock-full of lessons in kindness.'

Susie Hills, Founder of KindFest

'Everyone knows this stuff, but Graham says it in a way that sticks with you throughout the day. I keep *KIND* on my desk like a bedside book, as a beautiful reminder.'

Derek Sivers, author of Useful Not True

'An incredibly in-depth study into what makes workplaces – and people – truly kind and how to unlock that in your own working world. Essential reading for anyone wanting to transform their management style for a new generation.'

Lisa Smosarski, Editorial Director, The Stylist Group

'I was once told that if you can be one thing, be kind. Graham Allcott's excellent book is a timely reminder that kindness is an opportunity for everyone.'

James Reed, Chairman and CEO of Reed Group

'KIND is a handbook that champions kindness as the foundation of all that we do. Kindness should be at the core of every business, shaping a world where we feel safe to be our authentic selves and accomplish our best work. The more we can be true to who we are in our professional lives, the more impactful and joyful our world becomes. Graham's book serves as a playbook for leaders and organizations who want to make kindness their guiding principle. It demonstrates how putting kindness at the heart of your business not only drives profitability but also fosters positivity that extends far beyond the workplace. It's time for businesses to embrace kindness fully. Graham's book shows us how to do just that – making our companies kinder, more compassionate, and ultimately, more successful.'

Carlos Saba, Co-Founder of The Happy Startup School

'I have personally suffered at the hands of unkind leaders – people who, for whatever reason, think that yelling, selfishness, and throwing coffee cups is the right way to go. I wish they would read this book where Graham makes the case for kindness and lets us know how we can implement it in our lives.'

L. David Marquet, author of Turn the Ship Around

'This beautifully written and insightful book shows how you can make kindness your foundation for a happier and more rewarding life – at work and beyond. It weaves together compelling science, memorable principles and helpful examples – all in a warm, accessible and practical way. This is the timely dose of warmth and sanity we urgently need right now and shows how we can and must create a kinder world together.'

Dr Mark Williamson, Director of Action for Happiness

'Human sense meets business sense. A grounded, practical and generous book. Graham makes the case for kindness so well you can't help but turn towards it in everyday moments of work and life.'

Grace Marshall, author of Struggle

'This book reminds us that kindness is not just a virtue but a powerful competitive advantage in business.'

Lauren Currie, Founder and CEO of UPFRONT

'Simple, everyday acts of kindness can change the world, and are "rocket fuel" for collective enterprise. In KIND, Graham Allcott makes an utterly convincing case for kindness at work, in a blend of beautifully clear writing, well-researched scientific evidence, deep thinking and engaging anecdotes. A great read.'

Sally-Anne Airey, author of Mindful Command: The Way of the Evolving Leader

'I am so glad of Graham's wise and humane work. Rooted in the real world and full of genuinely useful advice, it's the antidote to hustle culture.'

Josie Long, Comedian & author

'At Pizza Pilgrims we put kindness at the heart of what we do. Not only is this the right thing to do from a human perspective – but we genuinely believe (and have evidenced) that it delivers commercially for the business and all our teams as well. It is great to see a book that champions this approach and celebrates the fantastic businesses that put kindness at the heart of their operation.'

Thom Elliot, Founder of Pizza Pilgrims

'I have learnt a lot during my 50 years in business...but the overriding thing is that "it is all about the people". You need to read this excellent book to understand what makes them tick.'

Julian Richer, Founder, Richer Sounds, Philanthropist & author

'In KIND, Graham gracefully captures the power of kindness in business and among its people. It is about nurturing our people through kindness and healing them along the way.'

Nand Kishore Chaudhary, Founder and MD of Jaipur Rugs

'Graham Allcott has written a wonderful book. It's a powerful, useful and moving work about how to improve your life and your work through something as deceptively simple as kindness.'

Frank Turner, Singer-Songwriter

KIND

The quiet
power of
kindness
at work

GRAHAM ALLCOTT

BLOOMSBURY BUSINESS
LONDON • OXFORD • NEW YORK • NEW DELHI • SYDNEY

BLOOMSBURY BUSINESS
Bloomsbury Publishing Plc
50 Bedford Square, London, WC1B 3DP, UK
29 Earlsfort Terrace, Dublin 2, Ireland

BLOOMSBURY, BLOOMSBURY BUSINESS and the Diana logo are trademarks of
Bloomsbury Publishing Plc

First published in Great Britain 2024

A catalogue record for this book is available from the British Library

Library of Congress Cataloging-in-Publication data has been applied for

ISBN: HB: 978-1-3994-1740-2; TPB: 978-1-3994-1737-2;
eBook: 978-1-3994-1739-6

2 4 6 8 10 9 7 5 3 1

Typeset by Deanta Global Publishing Services, Chennai, India
Text design by seagulls.net
Printed and bound in Great Britain by CPI Group (UK) Ltd, Croydon CR0 4YY

To find out more about our authors and books visit www.bloomsbury.com
and sign up for our newsletters

Dedicated to Elma Allcott, 29 July 1926 – 4 September 2023.

Kindness personified.

'PEOPLE WILL FORGET WHAT YOU SAID.

PEOPLE WILL FORGET WHAT YOU DID.

BUT PEOPLE WILL NEVER FORGET HOW
YOU MADE THEM FEEL.'

– MAYA ANGELOU

KIND

Graham Allco

CONTENTS

INTRODUCTION

Nothing distracts you faster from the emails on your phone than hearing your name called in the waiting room of Great Ormond Street Hospital with the words, 'We have a counsellor joining us for this meeting – is that OK?'

It was the spring of 2013; London was basking in its post-Olympic glory, the green shoots of economic recovery were starting to show and my own business, launched in 2009, was taking off. I'd just written *How to be a Productivity Ninja*, which would go on to become a bestseller. I'd even managed to get onto London's housing ladder and was ready to give this 'being a grown-up' thing a go. It felt like finally, all my years of working a bit too hard were starting to pay off. It seemed to be going so well, but here we were, in London's famous hospital for sick children, awaiting what would turn out to be very difficult news.

After being led into a tiny consultation room and the door closed ominously behind us, the doctor told us that our unborn baby had a unique chromosomal disorder. We all like to think of ourselves as unique, and every parent likes to think their baby is unique, but to Great Ormond Street Hospital, unique is *bad*. Unique chromosomes means there's no playbook for diagnosis, no trends and no predictability. Unique means they have to prepare for a range of scenarios; our baby might be born unable to breathe on his own, he might need 24-hour care his whole life, he might have severe disability, organ failure, heart problems, a small stomach, learning difficulties or all of the above. We didn't know what to expect and had only a short time in which to prepare for the worst and hope for the best.

The months that followed were some of the hardest of our lives. We nearly lost our baby at 21 weeks and were in hospital for tests so often that we joked about having a loyalty card. We had to quickly learn the lexicon of genetics: 'trisomy mutations' and 'mosaicisms' and 'long arms'. Nights were spent wide awake, worrying about the future, imagining the many scenarios and picturing how our lives would change.

Through the stress and anxiety of that time, between the hospital trips and sleepless nights, I continued to go to work, running my business, Think Productive. During this time I revealed to no one the pain and stress I was feeling; I kept a stiff upper lip and attempted to project the confident, self-assured leadership that I thought my employees expected of me (and perhaps also what I expected of myself).

On 30 October 2013, Roscoe was born surrounded by multiple midwives, doctors and surgeons, all braced for a child needing major patch-up surgery on entry to Earth. Thankfully, after a long checklist of scans and tests, they handed him to us, the major surgery they were expecting to have to perform no longer needed that day, but it was still the start of a journey full of challenges.

As I write this, we are in the middle of about a dozen major spinal surgeries that have somehow become routine. Our son has autism and developmental delay and some physical challenges too. It's fair to say he'll never play centre-forward for Aston Villa and allow me to live my childhood football fantasies vicariously through him. There are days when I grieve for the normal parenting experiences that we don't have with him. School sports days, birthday parties, Christmas concerts and family meals are often closer to ordeal than idyllic. But at the same time, oh my, what a gift he is.

Roscoe has taught me more about kindness than anyone else in the world. He is thoughtful and kind (and warm and hilarious and brave and engaging), but the magic happens because he's also a vessel for other people's kindness. When he gets invited to birthday parties, the invite invariably includes a text from the parent organizing it, asking if there's anything else they can do to make the space more autism-friendly for him – a small but vital act of kindness that fills my heart with gratitude every time. At his school, his differences and additional needs are not just accepted, they're celebrated. Watching the other kids encouraging him is heart-breaking in its inspiring simplicity. One of the biggest privileges in being his dad is witnessing all the kindness that he inspires. It's a reminder that we humans are naturally kind – we learn later in life, through conditioning and our own pain, how to bully and compete.

Kindness is many things. It's the man who gave up his seat for us on a busy standing-room-only train taking everybody home for Christmas. He recognized the meltdown Roscoe was having because of his own autistic child, whom he no longer had contact with and missed dearly. From that, the two of us struck up a beautiful and heartfelt conversation. Others joined in. Our rush-hour London stress fell away and I engaged in a deep and meaningful moment of connection with a stranger, all from a split-second moment of kindness.

Kindness is the busy staff in Costa Coffee taking time to indulge Roscoe's obsession with plastic trains. It is his teacher, every year, giving him a private tour of the new classroom on the training day, the day before term starts, and getting to know him in a quiet setting and so that he's more orientated in the noisy chaos the following day. Kindness is his teaching assistant, Rachel, putting ear defenders in his book bag to take home with him on November 5th, just in case he needed them for Fireworks Night.

The kindness that people show Roscoe is remarkable on its own, but it's the power of kindness to help us connect with and understand each other that is truly magical. And we *are* all connected: perhaps my greatest learning from parenting Roscoe is that I no longer see competition as the highest form of developed society – collaboration and interconnectedness are more beautiful and beneficial than the individualist narratives we are often fed.

As you'll see later in this book, we are all inspired, when we see or experience acts of kindness, to be kinder ourselves. It has a habit of melting our hard exteriors and snapping us out of the 'busy-ness trap', making us more open and available to deeper human connection and allowing us to experience the world in terms of 'glass half full'. But don't be confused into thinking this is all 'hippie stuff' – through its ability to connect and inspire, kindness helps us get things done, too.

The Quiet Power of Kindness

This book reveals the role that kindness can play at work and the extraordinary results it brings for leaders, teams and organizations around the world. I am sure when you think about your own experiences at work, you can think of examples of where either you or someone you worked for acted in a kind way and the positive effects that had. You'll have your own 'kindness role models' and I hope you aspire to be one, too. I know from my own 25 years-and-counting of experience as a manager, leader and business owner that placing an emphasis on kindness has played a critical role in my own success – in fact, one of the values of my company, Think Productive, is '*Trust and Kindness are our Rocketfuel*'. So why isn't there more kindness and why isn't everyone kind? It boils down to two simple truths:

1   **The role of kindness in business is misunderstood.** The prevailing narrative is that being a 'bastard' or thinking only of yourself is the most common route to unbridled success. The exact opposite is true: being kind is what naturally leads to better results.

2   **Kindness itself is misunderstood, and defining it more clearly helps it spread.** Kindness is strong, not weak. It's hard, not easy. It's what we do, not who we are. And let's be clear: 'kind' and 'nice' are not the same thing.

In Part One of this book, I'll start by challenging the idea that there is no place for kindness in business by taking a look at the science of kindness. We'll look at the extensive range of research across management theory, psychology, behavioural science and beyond to see how kindness drives higher results, better collaboration and much more. You will see the incredible benefits of being part of a team with kindness at its core and discover that the most caring leaders create a ripple effect of positive outcomes, from increased productivity to employee retention and beyond.

In Part Two we'll explore what I call the Three Myths of Kindness, so that we can help clarify what kindness is and isn't – because when we can clearly define kindness, it's much easier to make the case for more of it in our organizations, overcoming the biases and narratives that so often hold this back.

Kindness doesn't often make the headlines. It happens gently and quietly but leads to spectacular results. We always hear about stories of the business villains that get ahead – the fraudsters, dragons and strongman CEOs – now it's time someone told the story of leaders who care. This book will do just that.

The Art of Kindfulness at Work

In Part Three, we'll look at what it means to be 'Kindful'. 'Kindfulness' means doing as many kind things ourselves as we can, of course, but it's also about taking it a step further – moving beyond ourselves. To be 'Kindful' is to constantly ask ourselves the question: 'How can I create the spaces and opportunities for *other people* to express their kindness too?'. It means seeing kindness not just as something that we personally do, but as a culture that we help create that has the power to bring whole teams and organizations together. It is the assumption that there is always a kinder way to work if we help shape the culture that looks for it, even in the more challenging moments. In fact, even more so in the challenging moments.

And in Part Three we will move from the 'whys' to the 'hows' with the Eight Principles of Kindfulness at Work. Through the interviews and 'Kindness Hero' case studies, you'll see that there is no single way to be kind, but a multitude of approaches that you can pick and choose from, depending on the situation. Before we move on, allow me to quickly introduce you to the Eight Principles of Kindfulness at Work, which we'll come back to and explore more extensively in Part Three:

Principle One: Kindness Starts With You – We begin with the fundamental mindset shift that is needed to embrace Kindfulness as your superpower – that we can only truly be kind to others when we are kind to ourselves first. We have to be a role model for ourselves as well as those around us and practising kindness on ourselves puts us in the right mindset to be kinder to others, too.

Principle Two: Set Clear Expectations – Being crystal clear about our expectations (even if they are high) is central to an environment of psychological safety and trust. In leadership roles, it's about defining the three Vs: the **vision** for where you want to take people, the **values** that define and guide your decision-making and the culture, and the measurable **value** you want each member of your team to add. And whatever your role, these three Vs are the essence of a clear direction. Boundaries, feedback and communication are all part of a Kindful approach.

Principle Three: Listen Deeply – There is nothing kinder than giving someone your fullest attention and yet it can often feel like we're too busy or too embarrassed to listen with depth. This principle will teach you how to hone your empathetic listening skills so that you're able to tune into what's really going on.

Principle Four: People First, Work Second. Always – This has been a personal mantra of mine for many years. I created it to set the standard for how I wanted to manage people, especially when the shit hits the fan, but it has come to mean so much more. It's about recognizing peoples' need for dignity and honouring the humans that we all are outside of our work.

Principle Five: Be Humble – Great things happen at work when you don't care who takes the credit. When we focus on enabling others and 'being the spotlight, not the star', we encourage trust and teamwork. Humility – when we combine a confidence in our own skills with a generosity of spirit – is about getting out of the way of our own egos, in service of the team's happiness, development and performance.

Principle Six: Treat People the Way THEY Want to be Treated – It's often said that you should treat people the way you want to be treated but kinder still is when you treat someone the way *they* want to be treated. The true test of kindness is when your intention is matched by your impact and your kind gesture means as much to the person receiving it as it did to you giving it. I'll show you how to act with heart and help ensure that your impact matches your intent.

Principle Seven: Slow Down – The biggest source of accidental unkindness is busy-ness. When we slow things down, we unlock the compassion and empathy that our fast-paced culture often throws to the back of the queue. If we want to be curious about the needs of others, or make the time to put people first, we need to slow down and this principle offers practical ways to do just that.

Principle Eight: It Doesn't End With You – Kindfulness is more than just focusing on our own actions, it's also about building a culture or contributing to a team where kindness is encouraged and expected. Great leaders set the tone so that it doesn't even matter if they're in the room. Our final principle shows you, whatever your role, how to make work a place where everyone feels included and where kindness is encouraged, and how this in turn increases loyalty and motivation, as well as driving higher performance.

How to Make the Most of This Book

As you're about to find out, kindness is about actions, not just words, so this book is full of practicality and at the end of each chapter there are reflection questions for you to work through. I encourage you to use these reflections to really challenge yourself and embed the insights and principles.

At the end of each chapter there is also a Kindness Challenge. These challenges are some of my favourites, taken from my course on Kindfulness at Work. The challenges can be undertaken on your own, but you might also want to enlist a colleague or two and take the challenges together. Read a chapter each week, try the activities and tools in your work, take up the challenge for that week and then use the reflection questions to take stock or discuss with colleagues. There are free companion resources at www.grahamallcott.com/kindful for you to share with your team, too.

As you will see in Part One, Kindfulness gets results, but it is of course also an opportunity to change the world by bringing happiness to others. Over the years, both personally and professionally, I've come to see that through kindness, we can feel purposeful and more connected to one another. We can develop a sense of ownership, commitment and validation in our teams. We can swap the frenetic for the empathetic. Perhaps more surprisingly though, the subject of kindness can unlock all kinds of self-development opportunities. When we are forced to re-examine our relationship with kindness, with other people and with ourselves, it can sometimes be deeply uncomfortable and feel quite vulnerable. In my experience, some of the most profound learning comes from this place. So, I invite you to be open-minded to the insights and commit wholeheartedly to the challenges. Some might feel deceptively simple, others less so, but all have the propensity to push you out of your comfort zone. Don't be surprised if you're suddenly confronting some deeper life questions or personal truths through this work.

And finally, before we get started, a quick word of encouragement. There are thousands of other things you could be doing with your time and yet here we are. That says a lot about what you want from your work, from the world and the kind of life you want to lead. This journey might not always be smooth, but if you stick with it, I promise you that a fun, insightful and transformative experience lies ahead of us.

Let's get started.

'KINDNESS IS PROBABLY THE MOST IMPACTFUL ATTRIBUTE OF A HUMAN BEING – IT FOSTERS COLLABORATION, MOTIVATION AND INCLUSIVITY, AND IT'S WHAT MAKES YOU MEMORABLE AS A LEADER.'

JULIE BROWN, CHIEF OPERATING OFFICER, BURBERRY

Graham Allcott

PART ONE
THE CASE FOR KINDNESS

'Kindness fuels everything. If you're kind and people trust each other, then you win. It's as simple as that.'

It was October 2019 and I'd just delivered a keynote to a large investment bank in Rome. I was in the Q&A part at the end and someone asked me a question: 'Graham, apart from what you've outlined here about productivity, what's helped you build a global business from scratch over the last decade?' Perhaps you won't be surprised to hear that 'kindness fuels everything' was the first thing that came to mind.

In many ways, it felt so obvious to me that it doesn't need to be said, but I was immediately surprised at some of the pushback this answer received ('No way! Business is all competition!', 'The ruthless always succeed!'). There were a couple of people in the audience who seemed to have watched the 2013 Scorsese film *The Wolf of Wall Street* but had sadly taken it as an instruction manual for business success. Someone asked me to 'Look at Steve Jobs and Donald Trump!' as a reason why 'Kindness is surely for losers!'. But I also had lots of people rush to my defence, too, including Ray, the head of the team. Ray was the guy who had brought me in to deliver the keynote at his team's retreat. I knew his personal motto was 'Work hard and be humble' and I knew, just from my limited interactions with him as we briefed for my talk, that he was a remarkable leader – thoughtful, visionary, compassionate… and always about three steps ahead in anticipating what his huge team needed him to be.

Quickly, it felt like the room had divided into 'team kindness' and 'team screw-them-all-and-be-evil'. Luckily, even in the cut-throat world of investment banking, the majority seemed to be with 'team kindness', but it was fascinating to see the strength of feeling and the energy that had enveloped the room on such a seemingly harmless or soft topic as 'kindness'. It had been a high-stress 10 minutes at the end of my keynote, with the potential to derail my main message, but the signs were that I'd handled it well and it hadn't turned into a 'difficult day at the office' for me. Over lunch, I had as many people come up excitedly talking to me about kindness as they did about productivity.

I stayed in Rome for the weekend, eating incredible ice cream while staring at things built by the leaders of ancient civilizations. As I soaked up the sun-kissed autumnal beauty of the city, walking from human achievement to human achievement, I found myself reflecting on why kindness had divided the room during my Q&A. Why were some people so sceptical and hostile to something so useful and positive as kindness? Something so obviously good for the co-operation and survival of our species. And I reflected too on the business that I'd built, over many years, where kindness has always been integral to my approach. Somewhere near the Trevi Fountain, I resolved to write this book.

In Part Three of the book, we'll look at the Eight Principles of Kindfulness at Work and practical ways to bring kindness to wherever you work. Feel free to skip to there if that's what you're more interested in. But before that, it's important that we set the scene so what follows are some definitions of what kindness is and isn't, and some of the science. It's really a guide for how to talk about kindness and in particular, how to address the cynics you might know in your organization – the members of 'team screw-them-all-and-be-evil' – so that together, we can change some minds.

Why Kindness is a Win-win-win-win

The beautiful thing about kindness is that no one owns it and there's never a shortage. And not only is it free, but the more kindness you create, the more other people learn to create it too. Kind words cost nothing, and kind deeds have the power to strengthen the bonds between us, showing us that there's more in this life that unites than divides us. Organizations dedicate endless resources towards solving questions like 'How can we feel a greater sense of belonging?', 'How can we drive productivity?' or 'How can work feel more purposeful and our people more engaged?' The magic of kindness is already providing answers to these questions. It's time to shine a light on the incredible power of kindness.

In this chapter, we'll look at the myriad of benefits that kindness brings to people and organizations, and how kindness is a key driver of psychological safety in organizations – which in turn brings spectacular results. A kind act never has a single beneficiary. It's always a win-win. In fact, every single act of kindness is a win-win-win-win. Allow me to explain:

WHY KIND ACTS ARE A WIN-WIN-WIN-WIN

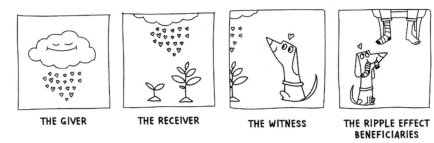

| THE GIVER | THE RECEIVER | THE WITNESS | THE RIPPLE EFFECT BENEFICIARIES |

Winner #1: The Giver

When we do something that brightens someone else's day, it usually brightens our own day too. Committing an act of kindness makes us, as the giver, feel good. Indeed, the science of kindness and what it brings to the giver is, on its own, a pretty compelling reason for kindness – before we even think about the wider benefits to the receiver and everyone else. Here are some of the main findings from studies looking at the science of kindness:

KINDNESS & THE BRAIN OF THE 'GIVER'

Studies have consistently found that our brain releases 'feel-good' chemicals when we are kind.[1] We receive a rush of oxytocin (the 'love hormone'). Oxytocin has the effect of improving empathy and trust,[2] and of course since an increase in empathy helps us see more opportunities for kindness, this becomes a self-perpetuating cycle. Oxytocin also has health benefits, such as lowering blood pressure and leads to a healthier cardiovascular system in general.[3] Increased oxytocin levels are also associated with an enhanced ability to read social cues, an increased ability to form social bonds and is beneficial for helping to combat depression.[4]

There are also links between kind acts and an increase in levels of dopamine.[5] Dopamine is our 'reward chemical', hence increased dopamine at work helps drive motivation and a sense of purpose. Studies[6,7] talk about the idea of a 'helper's high', where the satisfaction of solving a problem for someone else elicits a rush of dopamine to the brain. Dopamine is highly addictive, hence highly motivated people will be looking for their next dopamine hit, leading them either to more acts of kindness or more productive times at work. And if that wasn't enough, dopamine is also associated with feelings of happiness.[8] It's official – being kind makes you happier too.

Kind acts also help to lower anxiety. A study at the University of British Columbia[9] found that kind acts boosted levels of serotonin, with particularly strong effects on groups of people who identified as highly anxious. Serotonin is the 'mood hormone' and is associated with emotional stability, feelings of calm and also feelings of happiness. The study found that when a group of highly anxious people were asked to perform six acts of kindness each day, they saw a significant increase in positive mood after just a month. Their satisfaction in relationships improved and there was a decrease in their tendency towards social avoidance.

In the world of work, stress is often viewed as a natural and uncontrollable by-product of what we do. It's a big problem too: a recent Qualtrics study[10] found that in the UK, 90 per cent of people are stressed in their current job, with over 50 per cent saying they felt stressed 'most of the time'. Feelings of stress come from having too much of the stress hormone cortisol and we can lower our stress levels by lowering the levels of cortisol we have in our bodies. Studies have found that people who were kind on a regular basis had 23 per cent less cortisol in their bodies, having a significant effect on stress.[11]

But that's not all. Dr David Hamilton's book, *The Five Side Effects of Kindness*, lists a number of studies that show that kind acts make us fitter and healthier, too.[12] With organizations investing significant resources in employee healthcare and developing strategies to improve well-being and reduce sickness absences, kindness is an abundant but overlooked strategy. One study found that kindness led to fewer physical aches and pains in the body and that kindness slows the ageing process in the body. A study of people over the age of 55 found that those who regularly volunteered their time for at least two organizations were 44 per cent less likely to die early (and that's after sifting out every other factor, such as physical health, marital status, lifestyle habits such as smoking or drinking and so on).

Allan Luks' research[13] found that almost 50 per cent of participants reported feeling stronger and having more energy after helping others, with other positive effects such as feeling calmer and enhancing self-esteem also reported – all positive traits you would want in every member of your team.

Winner #2: The Receiver

The most obvious beneficiary, of course, is the person on the receiving end of an act of kindness. In research carried out by the Mental Health Foundation, 63 per cent of people said that being the beneficiary of an act of kindness had a positive influence on their mental health.[14] As we focus increasingly on mental health at work, something as simple as kindness can play a huge role in limiting the damage and make our working environment just a little bit more positive for our mental health.

When someone does a kind thing for us, it generally makes us happier too. It's that sense that someone has been thinking about our needs and that we're not facing all our challenges alone, and we're more connected to those around us. This happy effect of kindness has also been borne out in studies, too. A study in 2015[15] centred on asking 'givers' to spend 90 minutes performing small acts of kindness on people around them – things like holding open the door, handing out cookies, or writing cards with positive and supportive messages on them. The givers were asked to record the facial expressions of the receivers and unsurprisingly, it found that there was a higher instance of 'Duchene smiles' (sincere, all-face smiles) than a control group who didn't receive any kind acts.

A study of workers at Coca-Cola's Madrid headquarters[16] found that when people were on the receiving end of kind acts, they rated themselves as happier than a control group of those who didn't receive any kind acts. Participants reported big increases in feelings of well-being and positive attitudes towards their jobs. There was a heightened sense of camaraderie with other colleagues as people felt more connected and trusting of each other. The same study also reported a 'ripple effect' where beyond the control group, everyone else in the office felt higher levels of job satisfaction and life satisfaction, along with feeling more confident, more in control and with fewer symptoms of depression. It also increased motivation to 'pay-it-forward' and both givers and receivers felt more connected to their work.

Winner #3: The Witnesses

Simply being around kindness is good for us, too. If you've ever stood on a busy train and witnessed someone give up their seat for an older person, or make space to make it more comfortable for someone getting on in a wheel-chair, then you'll understand that the ripple effect of kindness is powerful. This is why teams led by Kindful leaders feel more close-knit and people feel a greater sense of camaraderie because they are spending time around regular acts of kindness.

In fact, witnessing a kind act is all it takes to see an increase in oxytocin and a reduction in stress levels.[17] A Harvard University Study examined the effects of witnessing kindness on the immune system and found some pretty astonishing results. The participants were asked to watch a 50-minute video of Mother Teresa as she carried out acts of kindness. They were then monitored for the levels of salivary immunoglobin A in their bodies. Saliva swab results found that there was a significant increase in salivary immunoglobulin A after watching the video and that the levels were still much higher even an hour after finishing the video. Salivary immunoglobulin A plays an important role in the immune system and is the body's first line of defence against harmful pathogens that are found in food. They labelled this 'The Mother Teresa Effect' – namely that even just witnessing acts of kindness brings us positive psychological and health benefits.[18] Similarly, a study team at Stanford University found that taking part in just a few minutes of loving-kindness meditation (where you dwell on the ideas of kindness and compassion to others) increased feelings of social connectivity and positivity.[19]

In the context of workplaces, this has a clear lesson: when we can shine a spotlight on acts of kindness going on within our teams, we are likely to improve the health and well-being of the entire office, simply by spending some time sharing these stories.

> 'THERE IS A BALANCE AND A FLOW TO KINDNESS.
> IT'S NOT ABOUT MINDLESS GIVING. IT'S ABOUT
> A CIRCLE, THAT RIPPLES OUT AND SPREADS.'
>
> **Emma Law, head of strategy, local government, UK**

Winner #4: The Ripple Effect Beneficiaries

Every day, opportunities to be kind present themselves to us. We are often too busy to notice them, or we feel we can't spare the time or bear the inconvenience they require to take action. Sometimes we feel a bit awkward or embarrassed so we choose the easier option and do nothing. Often we centre these decisions merely on 'us and them' – the giver and the receiver. However, usually in those quick mental calculations, we are neglecting the wider picture, because kindness has a ripple effect to it.

As we have just seen, the third winner (or winners) are the people who witness that act of kindness and experience that 'Mother Teresa Effect'. It increases their sense of well-being and even improves their immunity. And then that ripple effect of kindness continues apace. Kindness inspires more kindness. A lot more. The fourth winners from your single kind act are all the people who receive their own act of kindness, just because either the receiver or witnesses of yours were inspired to 'pay it forward' and do something kind.

A remarkable study in the *New England Journal of Medicine* centred on an anonymous 28-year-old who walked into a US clinic and donated their kidney to someone in need.[20] This single act of incredible kindness was found to have started a ripple spanning the length and breadth of the United States. Partners of beneficiaries and other family members who heard about the case were so touched and inspired by it that they then began to donate their own kidneys to other people in need. The report found at least ten people then received a new kidney as a direct consequence of that one original anonymous donor.

The receivers of smaller, more 'everyday' acts of kindness are also likely to be inspired to 'pay it forward', too. A study by the University of California[21] found that when one person gave a dollar, that simple gift inspired a knock-on effect, with additional generosity up to three times the original act. James Fowler, Professor of Political Science at the University, said of the findings: 'When people benefit from cooperation, they don't go back to being their old selfish selves.'

Even More Wins: Empathy, Trust & Psychological Safety

Above are the four main winners from a single act of kindness: the givers, the receivers, the witnesses and the beneficiaries of the ripple effect acts. But when we're talking about organizations, there is a bigger picture, too. Kindness creates a culture that is not only more satisfying to work in, but one that gets better results too. So, while it's of course powerful to see kindness as helping your team to be healthier, lower their stress levels, feel happier, improve their sense of connection to colleagues and feel more fulfilled at work, the organizational and cultural benefits go even further. The quiet power of kindness sets the tone for a culture of high-performance because:

- Kindness increases **empathy**, and empathy increases kindness.
- In this positive environment, there is more **trust** between individuals. These in turn help us to develop a sense of **'psychological safety'** (where people feel able to take the inter-personal risks that drive a whole host of other benefits).

THE GIFT OF PSYCHOLOGICAL SAFETY

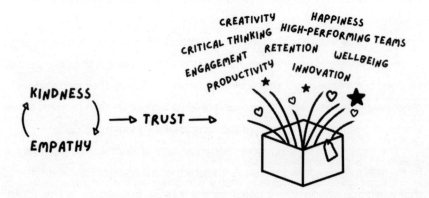

Creating and maintaining psychological safety should be one of your top priorities as a leader if you care about driving performance. It is the gift that keeps on giving because it allows organizations to look to everyone – not just those at the top – for the ideas, solutions and honest communication that pushes the work forward.

This is perhaps the pinnacle of what Tom Peters and Robert H. Waterman in their book, *In Search of Excellence*, describe as 'productivity through people'. Peters and his McKinsey colleague Robert Waterman's analysis of US corporations found a strong correlation between high performance and the organizations that placed a high degree of emphasis on treating people well, nurturing 'champions' and encouraging rank-and-file workers to share their ideas and improve quality. A recent report by the U.S. Chamber Foundation found that 88 per cent of employees felt that 'workplaces that are more accepting and kind are more successful',[22] and empathy, trust and psychological safety are important concepts to help us understand why. So, let's look briefly at empathy, trust and psychological safety in turn.

The Kindness and Empathy Loop

Empathy leads to more kindness and then kindness in turn leads to more empathy. I call this 'The Kindness and Empathy Loop'. When we truly care for people and take time to notice their needs (empathy), we naturally spot more opportunities to do good things for them. Of course, those are opportunities to be kind. It's worth noting that while those who are naturally more empathetic are generally found to be more kind too, empathy is not considered to be an innate trait and it can be learned and developed.[23]

A study in 2017 found that empathy was often diminished in the training of medical doctors and surgeons, but that through exercises that invited curiosity towards the needs of others, this could be increased over time. Here are five quick ways you can develop more empathy, in work and in life:

- Follow people on social media who don't share your political views. Ask yourself what might have led them to a place of such difference from your own views. Think about what they hold dear, and why.
- Volunteer your time for a good cause. Helping out at a local foodbank or homeless shelter is a great way to strike up conversations with people who don't share the same privileges or live the same kind of life as you. Along the way, you'll also meet other volunteers from all kinds of different backgrounds. Be curious about it: why are any of you there?
- Find a way to cut through the hierarchy at work. How can you have a deep conversation with someone on a very different pay grade to your own? What's going on in the lives of the boss or the most junior member of staff? Whether it's a work sports team, the smoking area, the taxi queue, the canteen or at a work social event, break outside of your bubble.
- Take people to lunch. Breaking bread together can be a window to the soul.
- Spend some time before a tricky conversation 'hypothesizing' so that you put yourself more firmly in others' shoes: what might they be expecting? What's it like to be on the other end of you? We'll talk more about this in Part Three (Principle 3: Listen Deeply) when we focus on listening (see also page 105).

I've found in my work that one of the best ways to develop more empathy is to practice being kind, or to experience the kindness of others. When people do kind things for us, or we experience the 'helper's high' as the giver of kindness (or even just feel that Mother Teresa Effect as a witness of kindness), it inspires us to pass it on.

Our brains search for the next hits of dopamine, oxytocin and other feel-good chemicals, and to do this, we start to think more about the needs of others

— so we are back to empathy again. This operates in a loop, where the more we think of the needs of others, the kinder we are, and the kinder we are, the more we think of the needs of others.

In my work with people around Kindfulness at Work, one of the first things I do is set them a 'Kindness Challenge'. The effects are profound as they slowly re-examine their relationships with others and with the world around them. But once the kindness and empathy loop kicks in, most people experience a rush of momentum and positivity. It can rewire our brains, too. This is because of the adaptability (neuroplasticity) of the brain. You may have heard of the 'Tetris Effect', which describes our ability to see patterns in anticipation of a future task (think of how you look at a wall when you've just finished playing the game Tetris). What I've found is that a Kindness Challenge encourages people to proactively look for the next kind act and in doing so, they dig a little deeper, to put themselves in the shoes of others. Thus, even the idea of kindness creates more empathetic connections. This loop is one of the fastest ways to build trust between people.

'TRUST IS THE GLUE OF LIFE. IT'S THE MOST ESSENTIAL INGREDIENT IN EFFECTIVE COMMUNICATION. IT'S THE FOUNDATIONAL PRINCIPLE THAT HOLDS ALL RELATIONSHIPS.'

Stephen Covey, author of *The 7 Habits of Highly Effective People*

Trust

Trust is a vital component of any collaboration and, indeed, any relationship. We can think of trust as a shortcut. Think back to any time you bought anything from a person or brand that you trusted — it's the trust built up over time that allows us to take action in good faith. It reduces the need for excessive due diligence. As Google's Head of Industry, Paul Santagata, once said: 'There's no team without trust.'[24]

In the PwC Annual Global CEO Survey of 2016, CEOs overwhelmingly said that trust and increased employee commitment to the organization were vital for performance. Fifty-five per cent of CEOs worried that a lack of trust was a threat to their organization's growth. A high level of trust makes employees more committed to staying with the company: a study found that 'feelings of warmth and positive relationships at work have a greater say over employee loyalty than the size of their paycheck',[25] while researchers at New York University found that 'the more employees look up to their leaders and are moved by their compassion or kindness, the more loyal they become'.[26] And it's not just team members, either: partners, suppliers, investors and customers are all people who you need to trust you.

Trust is even more important during difficult times – for example when managers are delivering uncomfortable feedback or having 'corrective conversations' with their employees. A 10-year study by the *Harvard Business Review*[27] found that leaders who expressed kindness found these conversations easier as they had built stronger relationships with their team members and had earned the 'right' to deliver the more difficult conversations because they had more trust in their relationships. The same study goes on to say that 'the number one thing holding back second-rate executives' is their 'inability to create trusting relationships'.

Trust takes time to build but can evaporate in seconds. It is the sum total of thousands of tiny actions that tell someone that you're clear what you stand for, and what you don't. So, from kindness and empathy, we build trust. Kindness is a brilliant opportunity to build trust in a safe way and show a more vulnerable, human and caring side of yourself, too.

Psychological Safety

Through kindness, empathy and trust, we create the conditions for psychological safety. This, in turn, creates remarkable results. The term 'psychological safety' originated in the 1960s and has been redefined for the modern era by the pioneering work of Amy Edmondson and Zhike Lei at Harvard Business School.[28] Whereas trust describes someone's personal opinion about someone else, psychological safety refers to what's happening in a team or group.

Edmondson defines psychological safety as 'The belief that one will not be punished or humiliated for speaking up with ideas, questions, concerns, or mistakes, and that the team is safe for interpersonal risk taking.'[29] In psychologically safe teams, team members feel accepted and respected. They also feel that they will be given the benefit of the doubt if they make mistakes.

One way to think practically about psychological safety is to think about the decisions we may make out of fear, or a lack of safety, versus those we can make when we feel psychologically safe. As we go about our day, often we face choices about whether to choose the more difficult path that gets us somewhere better or the easier path that shies away from what needs to happen. When we don't feel safe enough to take interpersonal risks, we choose the easier path.

A lack of psychological safety leads to thoughts like these:

- 'Everyone seems to be agreeing about this, but I just know something isn't right. I'd better not raise it, because I don't want to be the trouble-maker.'
- 'I can see he's unhappy with me, but I'd prefer to just move on than cause a scene.'
- 'I have a great idea for this, but it might be too controversial, or people might think I'm too whacky. It's not my project so I'll just keep it to myself.'
- 'That person always seems to get away with stuff, where other people get pulled up. It's one rule for them and another for everyone else. But what can I do?'
- 'I've already got so much work to do... But I'd better say yes to this new project they're asking me to do, even though I know deep down there's no way I could deliver it all on time. I'll just figure that part out later.'

In all of these instances, a lack of psychological safety means we shy away from killer questions, ideas or truths, for fear of the consequences. A commitment to truth – and commitment to bravely yet gracefully speaking the truth – is a fundamental aspect of good teamwork and good leadership. Kindness helps us prepare the ground for truth, as well as making uncomfortable truths easier to bear.

In studies looking at psychological safety and how to increase it, 'acts of kindness' are listed as one of the most significant factors. Several other factors are also important[30] although arguably, each of the following are also, in their own way, acts of kindness, too:

- role-modelling (which is kind because it shows those with less experience the way)
- encouraging the voicing of concerns (which is kind because of its commitment to ensuring people are heard)
- encouraging learning from mistakes (which is kind because it takes the emphasis away from blame and encourages more autonomy)
- increased knowledge sharing, transparency and a focus on inclusive leadership (all of which are kind because they promote respect and reduce the sense of alienation or exclusive hierarchy that can make work a miserable experience).

Psychologically Safe Teams are High-Performing Teams

Psychological safety is the gift that keeps on giving, not just creating an environment that people want to work in, but also driving high performance. In fact, a Google study over two years cited psychological safety as the number-one dynamic that sets its highest-performing teams apart,[31] and that it was four times more significant as a driver than things like individual performance, structure, clarity or meaning. Simply put, it matters much less who is on the team and much more how they each interact with the other members of the team. Teams with a sense of psychological safety are more productive, creative and innovative; decision-quality and critical thinking are enhanced; people are more engaged in their work and more loyal, as well as happier and less stressed. Suddenly kindness doesn't seem so 'fluffy' anymore, does it?

Boosting Productivity

Kindness and psychological safety boost productivity. A study for the University of Warwick found that kindness increased happiness and happier people ended up 12 per cent more productive than less-happy people.[32] The study also found that 'happier workers also use their time more effectively, increasing the pace at which they can work without sacrificing quality'.[33]

A study in Canada[34] found that organizations where kind behaviours were encouraged led to employees having 26 per cent more energy at work, that they are 30 per cent more likely to feel motivated and enthusiastic about acquiring new skills and being exposed to new ideas, and crucially, it led to a 20 per cent performance improvement compared with employees working in less civil or kind environments.

Kindness can feel subtle because it moves quietly. It is the small gestures – whether the adding of kind words to an otherwise difficult email, giving space for someone else to speak before you in a meeting, taking five minutes to check someone is OK, buying someone a coffee, or shining a spotlight on a job well done. These become the subtle glue that holds teams together. A leader's kindness and a team's sense of psychological safety can be hard to pin down to any one action and are experienced more as an attitude or general 'feeling'. There is a direct correlation between investing in people development and employee satisfaction[35] and end results. When Google increased their investment in employee support and training, job satisfaction rose by 37 per cent.

But when teams or workplaces become unkind, it's usually far from quiet or subtle. The *Harvard Business Review*'s 'Price of Incivility' study[36] found a clear link between toxic work environments and poor performance. Ostracism, incivility, harassment and bullying were shown to have a disastrous effect on productivity, as was the resultant burnout of staff, who then inevitably moved on.

The report used surveys from employees from a cross-section of industries to look at the performance effects of unkind behaviour. It defined unkind behaviour as including verbal abuse from a manager, passing on the blame for mistakes, talking down to others and other actions that led to people feeling psychologically less safe.

- Forty-eight per cent of people intentionally decreased their work effort as a result.
- Forty-seven per cent intentionally decreased the time they spent at work.

- Thirty-eight per cent intentionally decreased the quality of their work.
- Eighty per cent lost work time worrying about what had happened.
- Sixty-three per cent lost work time avoiding the offender.
- Sixty-six per cent said their performance at work had declined.
- Seventy-eight per cent of people said their commitment to the organization had declined.

Inspiring Innovation and Creativity

Kindness and psychological safety also help us think in better ways. One of the clichés of creative brainstorming sessions is the facilitator telling everyone, 'Don't worry, there's no such thing as a bad idea'. This is an important concept for creativity and innovation because it's an attempt to create a miniature form of psychological safety. By removing the prospect of judgement, people feel more able to share their ideas.

Interestingly, kindness has been shown to play a role not only in increasing psychological safety, which in turn creates the conditions for creativity, but also to directly stimulate creativity too. In the study of kindness at Coca-Cola (*see also* page 15), it was found that as the members of the team were encouraged to commit acts of kindness for each other, a sort of competitive atmosphere emerged, with each person trying to be kinder in the most unique or original way. Participants reported that this helped them to 'think outside the box' and flex their muscles as creative thinkers showing that thinking about ways to be kind helps people be more innovative.[37]

Improving Critical Thinking

Robust and rigorous critical thinking and clear communication are necessary to learn from mistakes, too. Studies have found that psychological safety plays a huge role in encouraging critical thinking.[38] Without it, such conversations can be too challenging as power dynamics and the fear of consequences encourage people to protect their own position rather than offer the harder insights that are necessary for learning or positive change.

Empathy and kindness therefore play a crucial role in helping organizations to have the tough conversations necessary to create better solutions.

One of the many downsides of a culture driven by fear and lacking psychological safety is 'group-think'. When you are afraid to speak up, it is much harder for diversity of thought to be present and much easier for the fear to drive convergence around the agendas or views of prominent people – often the HiPPOs, Avinash Kaushik's acronym for 'the Highest Paid Person's Opinion'.[39]

And as you will find out in Part Three, a Kindful approach will improve your ability to listen. Research has found that 72 per cent of award-winning projects involve talking to people who may be outside of the project lead's inner circle.[40] Simply put, casting a wider net for different perspectives and cherishing diversity of thought helps us to interrogate our ideas in a better way. Kindness and a care for people are crucial to building a strong network and multi-disciplinary teams.

Increasing Engagement and Retention

It's often said that people join organizations, but people leave bosses. The *Harvard Business Review* report 'The Price of Incivility' found that 12 per cent of people actually left their jobs because of the unkind behaviour of a boss or colleague. Kindness leads to psychological safety, but unkindness can be enough to break the entire relationship. It's shocking to think how much talent is wasted, simply because managers are unkind.

In recent years, there has been a higher focus on employee engagement as a key driver of performance. There are of course a number of factors that drive employee engagement – belief in the mission of the company, control and autonomy over your work and a sense of opportunity with regards to career progression being the obvious ones – but feeling connected to a community of peers is undoubtedly a huge motivator for all of us at work. Research[41] has found that teams with high employee engagement are 23 per cent more profitable than those with lower employee engagement. There was also on average 28 per cent less employee theft, 81 per cent less absenteeism and 64 per cent fewer accidents or safety incidents. The research found that kindness enhances employee engagement, but it also has the knock-on effect of making customers feel more engaged with the company and its services and products too.

One of the significant factors in employee engagement is the level of stress people feel in their jobs. Willis Towers Watson's Global Benefits report[42] surveying more than 22,000 employees across 12 countries found that there is a strong link between high stress and low employee engagement. Kindness, with its stress-busting hormones, is one of the quickest ways to tackle this. The same study found that only one in ten employees who reported low stress levels said they were disengaged. And unsurprisingly, the study found that highly stressed employees took nearly twice as many sick days as those who didn't feel stressed.

Disengagement is a significant issue that all organizations need to pay attention to, as well as being one of the most reliable predictors of low profitability and performance. The State of the Workplace report found that 85 per cent of employees are not engaged or actively disengaged at work, while Gallup research[43] finds that worldwide, only 13 per cent of people describe themselves as 'engaged' with their work. This disengagement is estimated to have a cost of $7 trillion per year in lost productivity. It's time we stopped accepting the narrative that work means the Sunday Blues and then living for weekends and holidays. We need to be a whole lot more ambitious about what work could – and should – look like.

Kindness, trust and psychological safety are therefore powerful tools in seeking to drive high performance, with APEX's 2012 Health and Well-being Survey finding that employees are 36 per cent more satisfied with their jobs and 44 per cent more committed to their companies when they are encouraged to express kindness at work.

When it comes to recruiting staff, a study from the University of Delaware[44] found that having a culture of kindness at work may attract employees to a company, allowing them to do their work with more compassion and leading to lower costs for recruitment and training, too.

Improving Happiness and Well-being

Central to any organization's success is the happiness and performance of the team. Kindness, empathy, trust and psychological safety can all play fundamental roles in making high levels of happiness and productivity not just an aspiration, but the cultural norm. The University of Sussex's 2021 research project, 'The Kindness Test',[45] is the largest-ever study of kindness. It found a direct correlation between people who said they gave, received or noticed acts of kindness with higher levels of well-being and happiness. And a *Journal of Social Psychology*[46] study found that performing acts of kindness resulted in increased life satisfaction.

High-stress companies in the US currently spend around 50 per cent more than average on employee healthcare and 550 million workdays are lost in the US due to stress.[47] Stress-related illnesses account for a staggering 80 per cent of medical expenses in the US. Organizations spend huge sums trying to reduce the stress on their employees, or instigating 'wellness programmes', whereas in fact, simple acts of kindness might be more effective in helping to reduce stress levels.

Acts of kindness lower our levels of cortisol and in environments where we feel trusted and safe, we are less likely to feel judged, out of control, wronged, or unable to raise concerns about safety or workload – all major sources of stress.

Of course the person best placed to know if someone is stressed, or to work out what they need to feel well is, of course, that person themselves. The reason people don't speak up about the pressure they are under, or their mental health taking a nosedive, is that they fear the consequences. Psychological safety is a vital aid to conversations about stress, well-being, mental health and the kind of workloads that are acceptable for each person to manage. Removing the undercurrent of judgement from those conversations, and building the confidence and safety to speak freely, helps us to get the best out of ourselves and each other.

KINDNESS HERO: CASE STUDY
OLE KASSOW, ENTREPRENEUR, DENMARK

Ole Kassow is an entrepreneur based in Copenhagen. He has started and run many businesses, including the global social enterprise, Cycling Without Age. When consulting for a bakery, Ole did 'kindness experiments', which he found to be a powerful way to build up loyalty and engagement from both customers and staff. He called in his employees and told them that he wanted them to give some products away for free, every day. There were no parameters other than to make sure the shop didn't go bankrupt.

Ole sat back and watched the results play out over a month. Some people used their new 'freebie superpowers' with their first customers in the day, others waited for someone who looked like they might be in need or having a bad day, while others looked for someone who was kind to them in order to 'return the favour'. Over the month, the average that each employee was giving away was a modest amount, equivalent to around £10 per day. After the experiment, Ole sat down with his team and asked them what they'd learned.

'The vast majority said that they felt it was so interesting,' he told me. 'Some said it was very hard because it really made them think who should have this bread, and you know, should I develop some criteria and so on. But above all, it made them far more interested in their job. They became far more engaged. Suddenly it wasn't just about handing over bread and taking in money and making a monthly salary. This was far more about understanding people and being interested in other people'.

Ole also asked his employees how they felt about their work and ran surveys to measure their happiness: 'We found that the people working in the bakery suddenly knew much more about their customers, they would engage far more in conversation with them. And there was a very significant increase in the way they felt about their job. So the emotion that they attached to being at work for four, six or eight hours had gone up very, very significantly, just by basically showing them the trust and saying, "You do this, but do it your way and then let us know what you feel about it."'

Kindness is the Best Marketing, Too

Kindness, as it spreads its feel-good chemicals, is of course a powerful tool to encourage the loyalty of existing customers and engage the curiosity of new ones too. It's easy to see why Ole Kassow's experiment in the bakery impacted customers as well as staff when we think of how many people received a little hit of oxytocin to the brain as a result of being the giver, receiver or witness when free bread and cakes were given out.

This is actually something I've experienced a lot personally. Whenever my son, Roscoe, and I go into a Pret A Manger, he seems to be doing something cute enough to warrant a free biscuit, or I'm offered my drink for free, which noticeably puts smiles on the faces of everyone else around us at the till, as well as dissipating the stress of the journey that I didn't even know was festering in my body. And of course, guess which shop I buy my cup of tea from next time I'm at the same station.

A business journal study from the Ritz-Carlton Hotel Company found that expressions of kindness created brand loyalty, drove customer engagement and forged long-lasting bonds.[48] And during the Covid-19 pandemic, Burger King received huge attention for using their social media platforms to profile the best dishes from local independent restaurants in an act of solidarity with their industry.[49] They even, at one point, encouraged their customers to order from McDonald's.[50] And brands like adidas and Carhartt received praise for pivoting to make gowns, masks and protective equipment for front-line medical workers.[51]

As consumer habits become more discerning and ethically-minded, 'ethical and kind' are becoming the 'new normal' in our purchases. How an organization treats its staff, how kind or unkind a supply chain is and how engaged those at the front desk appear to be with their jobs are all important signifiers. Arguably CEO Yvon Chouinard's motto of 'let my people go surfing' is as appealing to Patagonia's extremely loyal customer base as it is to the staff themselves.

I know this from my own business, Think Productive, too. Our MD, Elena Kerrigan, often says her aim is that our people 'sit in the pub and brag to their mates about working for us, rather than sit in the pub moaning about working for us'. Often when we are pitching to or onboarding new corporate clients, it's the fact that we've run a four-day working week since 2011, place a high value on kindness, or regularly measure happiness that gets the deal over the line. Our corporate value of 'trust and kindness as our rocket fuel' was meant to describe how, as a team, we treat each other, but it turns out that the rocket fuel extends to winning us more new business, too. And the opposite effect is true, too. The 'Price of Incivility' report from 2019[52] found that, in dealing with unkind behaviour, 25 per cent of employees took out their frustration on the customers.

THE CASE FOR KINDNESS IS CLEAR

The science confirms what we instinctively know: that kindness, whether we are the giver, receiver or even just the witness, can have a profound effect on our lives and work. And that the empathy, trust and psychological safety that it generates means it becomes the gift that keeps on giving at work. Now, I want to bust what I see as the three big myths of kindness and then later, in Part Three of this book, I'm going to show you how you can develop a mindset of Kindfulness to improve your workplace. But before we do that, as will happen at the end of each chapter, I want to turn this over to you.

Over to You

At the end of each chapter, I'll be leaving you with two things:

- Questions for Reflection
- The Kindness Challenge

As with all books like this, the real learning is in taking action and then reflecting on what happens so please don't skip these bits!

For the Questions for Reflection, feel free to start a new notepad, or make notes somewhere in your phone.

For the Kindness Challenge, if you'd like to, you can see each challenge as being a 'weekly challenge' and embark on what I expect will be a journey of deep personal growth. What you will find is that although kindness can appear 'soft' or subtle, the effects of exploring kindness can lead to some profound shifts, so strap in.

Questions for Reflection

- Who in your life have been your kindness role models?
- When have you used kindness in your leadership or in how you interact with others?
- What effect did it have?
- Can you think of a moment where you missed the mark? What were the circumstances that contributed to this? What were the outcomes?
- As we start this process, if you had to rate yourself on a scale of one to ten (where one is unkind and ten is kind), where would you be?

Now, imagine a year from here and you've moved one point up that scale…

- What does it look like? Can you think of particular habits that are different?
- What small actions can you now take towards that goal?

Kindness Challenge

This first challenge is a simple one. This week, commit one act of kindness each day in line with your authentic self. These can be random acts of kindness you do for a stranger, or intentional acts of kindness within the context of your workplace, family or community. They can be radical and spectacular things or tiny moments of quiet kindness. The important thing is to notice what happens when you're kind.

Make a note of the emotions that come up for you as you experience these acts of kindness, what you observe is happening for the receiver and any feedback they offer you. If any of these acts of kindness lead you towards opportunities for a conversation about them (with the person involved, or with your colleagues), then be brave and start that conversation.

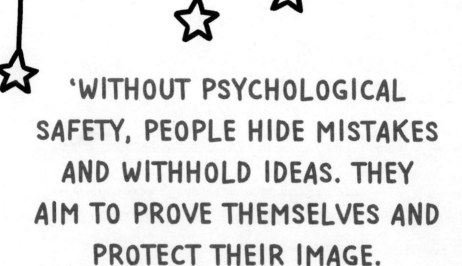

'WITHOUT PSYCHOLOGICAL SAFETY, PEOPLE HIDE MISTAKES AND WITHHOLD IDEAS. THEY AIM TO PROVE THEMSELVES AND PROTECT THEIR IMAGE.

WITH PSYCHOLOGICAL SAFETY, PEOPLE ADMIT ERRORS AND VOICE SUGGESTIONS. THEY STRIVE TO IMPROVE THEMSELVES AND PROTECT THEIR TEAM.'

ADAM GRANT, ORGANIZATIONAL PSYCHOLOGIST AND BESTSELLING AUTHOR

Graham Alla

PART TWO
THE THREE MYTHS OF KINDNESS

The previous section of this book, Part One: The Case for Kindness, shows us the weight of science in support of the role that kindness can play at work. The more you care, the more you drive the trust and psychological safety that are responsible for high performance in organizations. But there's a problem. We know that there could be a lot more kindness at work, but often, it's the unkind, self-serving and toxic behaviours that seem to win out. That's because despite all the science, how we think about kindness is often wildly misunderstood. Kindness can be misconstrued with and mistaken for lots of other less desirable traits and it's time to correct some of those false narratives. Here, we will focus on what I call The Three Myths of Kindness and show you why they are so misguided. The Three Myths are:

- **The Evil Genius Myth.** In other words, 'being a bastard is how you succeed in business'.
- **The Pushover Myth.** This is the idea that 'kindness is weakness'.
- **The Do-Gooder Myth.** The notion that 'there are kind people and unkind people and there's not much we can do about it'.

By debunking these myths, we can achieve a more enlightened understanding of kindness, both for ourselves and for the people we lead so let's start with the myth that came most loudly from members of 'team screw-them-all-and-be-evil' when I talked about kindness at my client keynote in Rome.

Myth One: 'Being a Bastard is How You Succeed in Business'

It was just after 5 p.m. Pacific Time on 9 May 2008 and Justin Maxwell had had enough. He sent a resignation email to his boss and walked out of his office, never to return. The recipient was Elizabeth Holmes, charismatic founder of Theranos, one of the most hotly-tipped companies in Silicon Valley at that time. Maxwell's email to Holmes was a snapshot of the relentless, cut-throat culture that pervaded Theranos:

'I wish I could say better things, but I think you know exactly what is going on at Theranos and choose to either support it or ignore it and therefore support it implicitly. Lying is a disgusting habit, and it flows through the conversations here like it's our own currency.

'The cultural disease here is what we should be curing, and I truly believe if you had wanted to change it, the three seniors would have been reprimanded, sent to managerial training, and taught how to behave in a cooperative environment months ago...'[1]

Holmes was a young entrepreneur with a big vision to revolutionize blood-testing and disease diagnosis by offering a multitude of tests via one machine and a single pinprick of blood. With her distinctive low voice and piercing eyes, she was a master storyteller but what she failed to say was that the technology didn't live up to her promises and in January 2022, she was found guilty of conspiracy to commit fraud against her investors.[2]

Holmes's story has been well-told via news coverage of the trial, as well as in TV series, podcasts and biographies, most notably John Carreyrou's award-winning biography, *Bad Blood* (2018). Carreyrou talks about a working culture that certainly couldn't be described as kind:

'Would-be whistle-blowers were threatened with lawsuits. Criticism of leadership or practices was unwelcome. Those who pushed back were usually either fired or marginalized to the extent that they had to leave – they had an expression, which was to "disappear" someone. The paranoia went into overdrive.'[3]

Perhaps one of the less-talked about and more uncomfortable truths of the Theranos scandal is that it highlights just how seduced we can be by the idea of a 'genius entrepreneur saviour' and their quest to 'change the world'. It's a long lineage, which Holmes seemed conscious of, as she deliberately tried to cast herself as the next in line. Dressed in a Steve Jobs-style black polo-neck sweater, holding up one of her blood capsules the way Steve used to hold up a new iPhone on magazine covers, Holmes cultivated a slick personal image. She emphasized that she was a Stanford dropout just like Bill Gates, Steve Jobs and Mark Zuckerberg before her and even called one of her devices the 'Edison'. By the time she appeared on the cover of *Forbes Magazine* in 2014, with the headline 'This CEO is out for blood', Holmes was an industry star. She also emulated some of the aspects of confrontational and toxic culture that pervaded the accounts of Jobs' working practices, such as pitting teams of researchers against each other, with the losing team being fired.

The trope of the unruly genius entrepreneur who isn't required to play by the same ethical rules as the rest of us still captures the imagination today. From Elizabeth Holmes to Elon Musk, Jeff Bezos to Donald Trump, the idea that society needs to tolerate the bad or unusual behaviour of an evil genius because 'that is just part of how they get the job done' is one that we must challenge. Emulating Steve Jobs' famous short temper or aggressive people management skills doesn't mean you have the next Apple on your hands. And as the case of Elizabeth Holmes clearly shows, far from being the blueprint for success, more often than not it doesn't work out too well.

The 'Business Bastard' Continuum

Shark Tank. Dragons' Den. Gordon Gekko's 'Greed is Good'. Mr Burns in *The Simpsons. The Wolf of Wall Street.* The Fyre Festival... Right back to Shylock and Ebenezer Scrooge, media and fiction love the idea of the 'Business Bastard' – the archetype of the successful mogul or evil genius hyper-capitalist who is greedy, selfish and happy to ruthlessly win at the expense of others.

The narrative prevails that being successful comes from shouting at people, screwing them over and being unkind. The assumption is that there's a direct correlation between our propensity for unkindness and for success and wealth. When we see the worst kinds of behaviour rewarded with money and success, we perhaps assume that those people are just the ones prepared to indulge a little more of the darker parts of their soul than we were. They were simply more ruthless than we were prepared to be, hence why they were more rewarded. We assume that business is war, it's 'dog eat dog'; that those who rise to the top echelons of success do so with the highest body count. Of course, our operating context in recent times has been a form of capitalist economy that is increasingly aggressive and competitive so subconsciously, people assume these forms of behaviour must be the things that bring about success. Less kindness equals more success. More kindness equals less success … right?

Wrong. In fact, the opposite is true. As Part One, The Case for Kindness, shows us, Kindful leaders achieve huge successes all the time, it's just that their behaviour is mostly much less cinematic or fascinating as they quietly go about the business of looking after their staff, empowering others around them to help them succeed and benefit from the law of reciprocity.

THE BUSINESS BASTARD CONTINUUM

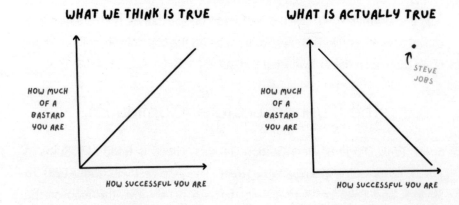

Duncan Bannatyne is one of the UK's most successful entrepreneurs, having built a £100m+ fortune from scratch. He was even one of the stars of the BBC's *Dragons' Den* show for many years:

> 'I'm immensely proud to say that I've achieved everything without being ruthless. You don't need to be ruthless in business. All I ever did was buy land at a price other people wanted to sell it for, give builders a contract at a price they suggested and then people used my services at a price I advertised them at. What's ruthless about that? I've also done a lot of my work in industries – nursing homes, day nurseries and health clubs – that have made life better for people. Business really, truly isn't about being ruthless. Single-minded, sure, but ruthless? No way.'[4]

And *Dragons' Den* entrepreneur Nick Jenkins, the founder of Moonpig.com, told me he had no interest in living up to the 'business bastard' archetype when he told people he didn't like their business during his time on the show:

> 'I think you can still force people to question their own business model without having to be brutal about it. I mean, the brutal bit is realizing that your own business model is awful. Actually, then you beat yourself up about it. You just have to point out what's wrong with the business idea. And that's enough.'

It's worth us remembering a few things:

- **Correlation isn't causation.** Just because Donald Trump boasted about being ruthless on *The Apprentice* doesn't mean that it was this characteristic that was actually responsible for his success. It probably also had something to do with the substantial loans his dad gave him.
- **It isn't the whole story.** The currency of cinema, fiction, news and social media is attention and storytellers achieve success by sensationalizing or exaggerating the facts so that we are more fascinated by the story they're trying to tell. And all archetypes, including the 'business bastard' archetype, are shortcuts to get us

to the story as quickly as possible, meaning that depth and nuance are sacrificed.

- **Baddies are naturally more interesting characters than goodies.** This is because for the vast majority of us, baddies seem more alien or unusual to ourselves, so there's a fascination about what motivates them and how they came to lose their scruples. Perhaps if we are really honest, we are also curious about what it would take for us to entertain the thoughts of our own 'shadow selves'.

- **Survivorship bias means we forget all those whose bad behaviour *didn't* lead to stunning business success.** Archetypes and clichés have a habit of reinforcing themselves via confirmation bias. Over time, as businesses fail, they are forgotten and so the negative results of unkind behaviour are less visible.

- **Occasionally, there's a high-profile outlier.** Steve Jobs is often cited as the proof of the rule that 'business bastards win', whereas he's actually the exception to the rule that 'kinder people win'. Even so, surely it was his incredible vision for design that made him successful, not his ability to shout at colleagues in meetings?

- **There are examples of leaders who are known for being incredibly kind.** Investor Warren Buffett is far more successful than former Wall Street trader Jordan Belfort (the original 'Wolf of Wall Street'). He inspires incredible loyalty from his staff and getting kind words from Buffett in the annual report is seen as a rite of passage for Berkshire Hathaway executives but these aspects of his persona are often overlooked because they're less interesting than how much Coke he drinks or the old car that he still drives. And let's not forget that Buffett is the biggest philanthropist of all time, deliberately doing so quietly by investing predominantly through the foundation named after his friends Bill and Melinda Gates.[5]

It's time we challenged this deep-seated narrative, which is damaging so many of our business institutions and causing untold misery in human lives. And yes, for the sake of profitability too, it's time we rewired our brains to what the quiet truth really is:

More kindness equals more success.
Less kindness equals less success.

There are also plenty of studies that point to being likeable as a key ingredient for success, too. For example, a *Harvard Business Review* study profiled 51,836 leaders and found a direct correlation between how likeable someone is with how effective their leadership was deemed to be. Just 27 of the leaders who were in the bottom quartile for likability were in the top quartile for effectiveness. That means you have about a one in 2,000 chance of being a successful leader if you're unkind. Unkind leaders achieved lower engagement from their staff, lower effort and higher turnover.[6] Studies such as these and many others help bust one of the most common myths around kindness. There is absolutely a place for kindness in business. Moreover, its place is at the leading edge of success.

But isn't life 'Dog Eat Dog' and All About 'Survival of the Fittest'?

The 'business bastard', we are told, lives in a world where 'business is war' and it's 'dog eat dog' and where human nature is characterized by greed above all else. Of course, this too is an over-simplification. Even the Father of Capitalism, Adam Smith, takes issue with this idea that violent competition is the natural order. Smith is often quoted from his magnum opus, *The Wealth of Nations*, as saying, 'It is not from the benevolence of the butcher, the brewer or the baker that we expect our dinner, but from their regard to their own interest'[7] but contrary to popular belief, even he was not in favour of the 'Survival of the Fittest' approach. In *The Theory of Moral Sentiments*, Smith argues, 'To feel much for others and little for ourselves, to restrain our selfish and to indulge our benevolent affections constitutes the perfection of human nature.'[8]

Of course, competition and competitive advantages can be extremely profitable, but co-operative behaviours are a huge part of the way we work. Whether it's finding a win-win instead of a win-lose solution in negotiations, working in partnership with the same organizations with which you also sometimes compete, or spending time and effort helping out the people around you, there are many ways to drive performance that require a focus far beyond personal greed or win-lose.

'BEING UNKIND IS A TAX ON YOUR TALENT – IT WILL WEIGH DOWN YOUR POTENTIAL.'

Steven Bartlett, entrepreneur and host of the podcast,
The Diary of a CEO

The (Fictional) Art of Corporate Warfare

In the 1960s, Sun Tzu's ancient text *The Art of War* became a global business bestselling book. Popularized by consultants working in some of America's biggest corporate companies, the text has permeated every part of working life, even down to the language we use. We talk about our 'mission statements', 'touch base' and 'rallying the troops'. We 'take the flak' or get 'caught in the crossfire', hoping that one day our strategy means we 'make a killing'. Microsoft's former CEO Steve Ballmer famously said, 'I bleed Microsoft.'[9]

Ironically, *The Art of War* wasn't written as a manual for war at all but a manual for peace. Michael Nylan is a translator who has studied and translated the classic text. He writes, '*The Art of War* might as well be named *The Art of Life*, since it famously advises readers (originally all-powerful men at court) to avoid war, by any means, if possible, on the two cogent grounds that it is far too costly a substitute for diplomacy and that the outcome is never assured, given all the variables at play.'[10] Yet in the hands of corporate strategists, the text became co-opted as a handbook for corporate warfare.

There are other narratives that I think describe much more accurately the endeavours of most twenty-first-century work:

- **Business as science:** We follow a process of hypothesis, experimentation, continuous improvement and advancement.

- **Business as art:** We invent, create, problem-solve and come up with new ways of looking at things.
- **Business as service:** We devote our attention to someone else's needs and help fulfil them.
- **Business as a game:** We try to master new skills, get to the next level and become better than we were before.
- **Business as cabaret or circus:** Where people come together to curate and experience a variety of exciting things that enrich our lives.
- **Business as change-making:** We collaborate to fix what's wrong with the world.

Exercise: Spot the Corporate Warfare Bullshit

You might be surprised just how much *The Art of War* and militaristic analogies pervade our working culture. Use this Business War-Room Bingo Card to raise awareness among your colleagues as to just how prevalent this can be:

THE BUSINESS WAR-ROOM BINGO CARD

RETREAT	TOUCH BASE	RALLY THE TROOPS	TAKE THE FLAK
MISSION	IN THE TRENCHES	PLAN OF ATTACK	BITE THE BULLET
GUERILLA MARKETING	A MINEFIELD	STRATEGY	COUNTER-OFFENSIVE
SLAYING IT	CAUGHT IN THE CROSS-FIRE	MAKE A KILLING	ON MY RADAR

Even if We Can Conclude That Business Isn't a War, Aren't We as Humans Inherently Selfish?

William Golding's *Lord of the Flies* is a great work of dystopian fiction, often cited as indicative of humanity's inherent selfishness, but the Dutch historian Rutger Bregman, in his book, *Humankind: A Hopeful History*,[11] tells the story of when a real group of people found themselves in a real-life situation of abandonment on a deserted island, off the coast of Australia. They behaved co-operatively not competitively, developed democratic systems and made their collective strength greater than the sum of their individual skills – even to the point of mending a broken leg without medical training. And yet these fictional narratives and archetypes resonate in our culture so much louder than the truth.

'NO ONE HAS EVER BECOME POOR BY GIVING.'

Anne Frank

The Source Code for Kindness: Abundance

'Business as war' derives itself from a scarcity mentality: the belief that it is necessary for companies and individuals to fight over ever-thinner slices of the pie rather than work together to grow the pie. This has been the dominant narrative in recent decades, even during long and sustained periods of economic growth. But, there are a number of trends that could move the economies of the world towards more of an abundance mentality over the next generation or two. The rejection of conspicuous consumption in favour of more sustainable consumer behaviour, the rise in calls for a Universal Basic Income, increasing automation of existing job roles resulting in higher standards of living for more people, more flexible working patterns ... all of these point towards an economy where basic needs are met, and where services replace goods as the mainstay of consumer happiness. Over time, we can imagine this leading to growth in service sections of the economy that support happier and healthier lifestyles, such as leisure, fitness, mental health and counselling services, well-being and learning, all of which still require human interaction. As time goes on, it's likely that it will be become even less acceptable to behave as a 'business bastard'.

An abundance mentality – the belief that there is, ultimately, enough to go around – is a vital precursor for our kind thoughts and actions. Later on, we will discuss the concept of abundance much more, but for now, I invite you to reflect on the 'abundance vs scarcity' dynamic with these three simple questions:

- What do you think Jeff Bezos or Elon Musk really want?
- What would your life look like, in specifics, if you had 'enough'?
- If you think about the gap between 'right now' and 'enough', how much of that gap is real versus imagined?

Myth Two: 'Kindness is Weakness'

If you're just kind to everyone, doesn't that make you a pushover? It's a common question I hear. It's important to be clear about what we do – and don't – mean by kindness. Genuine kindness could not be further from weakness. Kindness is lending someone a little bit of your strength instead of reminding them of their weakness. It's rarely the easy option, either: it requires confidence, courage and the skills to be able to navigate uncomfortable emotions and communicate with clarity. Kind isn't weak, it's *badass*.

'KINDNESS IS WILDLY UNDERRATED IN OUR CULTURE AND IS MISUNDERSTOOD AT TIMES AS WEAKNESS, WHEN IT'S THE ULTIMATE STRENGTH.'

Gary Vaynerchuk, entrepreneur and bestselling author

There are times in leadership when we have to face really challenging obligations. Giving people difficult feedback, breaking bad news, firing people … these are all situations that require a commitment to truth in order to drive them through and a commitment to delivering them with a level of grace that limits the damage.

General Stanley A. McChrystal, former head of the US Military, told me about the day he got fired by former US President Barack Obama: 'I will say that what was clearly the most difficult day in my life, he didn't make it any more difficult. He did something that he thought he had to do. And, I would have preferred he did it differently, but I respected his decision. And he did it with a level of class and compassion that is what a President ought to have. And so I walked out of there, appreciative of that. You know, still in shock. But there are a lot of ways you can do things in life, there's a lot of ways you can treat a waiter at a restaurant, or someone who does some interaction with you. And you get a choice in every interaction, whether to show kindness and class, or not.'

Nice vs Kind

Kindness gets a bad press sometimes because it's confused with 'just being nice'. 'Kind' and 'Nice' are not the same. In fact, there's a world of difference between 'Nice' and 'Kind' – and I would go as far as to say that they're closer to being opposites than they are to being the same. 'Nice' can often be weak. 'Nice' means telling people what they *want* to hear, whereas 'Kind' means telling them what they *need* to hear.

People are 'Nice' when they want to be liked. Niceness can also be unfocused, or lacking in discipline or strength. Nice people avoid conflict or difficult feedback and focus on people-pleasing and everyone being in harmony, which means when things are going well for your team, nice people add as much value as kind people. But when things are tough, nice people often crumble under the pressure. This is when kind people reveal their strength even more – and it's often in the hardest times that the kindest people help everyone else through.

NICE VS. KIND

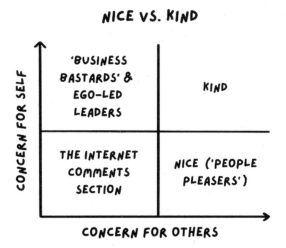

Nahla Summers is the founder of Sunshine People. Every year she undertakes world record challenges, like travelling 5,000 miles on a stand-up ElliptiGO bike, encouraging people not to donate money but to 'sponsor' her through kind acts towards others. Her work is about spreading cultures of kindness. Nahla ran a session for one of my Kindful Leadership groups, and she posed a question that told us a lot about the difference between 'Nice' and 'Kind':

> Imagine you're in a rush on your way to work and part of your routine on your journey is to get yourself a morning coffee and pastry from your favourite local coffee shop. This one particular day, you approach the doorway of the coffee shop and see a homeless man sitting outside the coffee shop, begging. You walk into the coffee shop, but you keep thinking about how his blanket doesn't seem warm enough for this weather and what a terrible time he must be having so when you get to the counter, instead of ordering one coffee and one pastry, you order two of each and you give him the coffee and pastry on the way out.

Is this a kind act? On the surface, it appears to be. But what if the man had just had a coffee already, or he didn't like coffee, or was allergic to pastries, or just wasn't hungry? Then the impact of this action doesn't match its intent.

Genuine kindness needs to meet the other person's needs, not just assuage your feeling of guilt for being warm and comfortable in your life while others are not. A truly kind act would have been to sit with that man, even for a few seconds, on your way into the coffee shop. Ask him how he's doing. Treat him as a human, not just one of 'the homeless'. Help him feel seen before you see if you can help. Here, what was missing was the empathy and the result was an action that was Nice, but not Kind. Let's look at how 'Nice' vs 'Kind' might play out in a typical meeting:

Situation	'Nice' reaction	'Kind' reaction
Someone needs to receive some feedback about the impact of their behaviour or poor performance.	Avoid giving this feedback in case it hurts the person's feelings.	Tell the truth, but in a way that makes clear you're FOR the person. Make it clear you're not talking about them, but their actions.
Disagreement	At the time: Keep your opinion to yourself. Nod along, give a 'dirty yes' in agreement After the meeting: bitch about the person or situation quietly to colleagues.	Disagree, but with respect. Say no if you mean no. Work with the person/ people who oppose you to explore it.
Running out of time	Overrun so that everyone's contributions are heard extensively.	Acknowledge and respect the time constraint first. Renegotiate the finish time, OR respectfully ask people to keep their contributions short and avoid repetition.
Communicating a decision already made that's likely to be unpopular.	Talk about the decision vaguely in a dozen different ways, but without ever getting to the point. End result: lack of clarity about what the decision actually is.	Start by addressing the decision directly, in the clearest possible terms, acknowledging that it's not a popular decision and lead discussion about peoples' concerns.

The Salted Caramel Test: Truth & Grace

If you're still struggling to see the difference between 'Nice' and 'Kind', you can think about it like this. At some point in your career, you'll have heard a colleague or friend say 'the trouble with X is that they're too nice'. Whereas the only time someone says 'you're too kind', it's as the warmest compliment.

Christina Kisley is an organizational development coach who has worked with some of the US's leading C-suite executives for the last 30 years. Her definition of kindness is that it's a mixture of 'truth and grace'. You're *for* the person and you act respectfully and with care and compassion towards them, but you're also committed to truth and not afraid to shy away from the truth of what they need. Kind people have the difficult conversations because it's the right thing to do.

One of the easiest ways to tell the difference between 'Nice' and 'Kind' is what I call the Salted Caramel Test. Salted caramel is, of course, the best food humanity has ever created (along with the biscuit equivalent, chocolate HobNobs). But why is salted caramel so addictive? Caramel on its own tastes nice, but the sweetness very quickly becomes sickly. Salt brings purpose and flavour to all kinds of foods, but on its own is unpalatable and even if slightly overdone, salt ruins the food. But when we have salt and caramel together in the right combination, it's another world entirely.

This is the difference between 'Nice' and 'Kind'. Kindness is the salted caramel of human behaviour. It's the 'truth and grace' together that is hard to resist. The 'truth' helps get things done and helps people learn. The 'grace' allows us to bring those difficult truths to the table in a caring way, creating a virtuous circle where that person then feels empowered and expected to speak their truth (with grace), too.

'Nice' cultures shy away from the truth and inevitably over time, this leads them too far from purpose. Unkind or aggressive cultures that focus only on purpose don't get the best out of people and risk implosion. Kindful cultures encourage the communication and care that builds empathy, trust and psychological safety.

David Bradford is one of the founders of Stanford University's most popular MBA elective module, Interpersonal Dynamics – also affectionately referred to as 'the touchy-feely course'. I interviewed him and co-founder Carole Robin and asked them, with their decades of collective experience working with some of the brightest and best business leaders in the world, what kindness meant to them. David paused for a moment and said, 'I worked with a guy, Geoff, who was a vice president at a large electrical firm. Geoff's department had missed his targets for two quarters in a row. At a company offsite, his boss asked him for a quiet word and they went off away from the group to chat. He said to Geoff, "You know I love you, but I really can't have a third quarter missing targets here. If that happens, you know I'm going to have to make a change, don't you?"'

His boss's words were direct and the consequences of them were immediately clear. David told me: 'Of course, his department made target that following quarter and that story always stuck with me as a really good example of being kind – you have to care enough about someone to say the very worst thing they could hear, but do it in a way that they know you're on their side, too.'

KINDNESS HERO

KINDNESS HERO: CASE STUDY
JACINDA ARDERN, FORMER PRIME MINISTER OF
NEW ZEALAND: 'PLEASE, BE STRONG AND BE KIND.'

It was 21 March 2020 when Jacinda Ardern delivered her Prime Ministerial broadcast to a frightened New Zealand. Covid-19 risked spreading through the country: 'I ask that New Zealand does what we do so well. We are a country that is creative, practical and community minded. We may not have experienced anything like this in our lifetimes, but we know how to rally, and we know how to look after one another, and right now, what could be more important than that? So thank you for all that you're about to do. Please, be strong, be kind and unite against Covid-19.'[12]

Jacinda put 'minimizing harm to lives and livelihoods' at the centre of her approach to the pandemic. Unlike many leaders around the world, she didn't attempt to shy away from the fear and unknown of the time and she didn't plant false hope. Instead, she focused on putting kindness and humanity at the centre of her response. When a journalist asked her how she felt, she said, 'I'm not worried, because we have a plan.' She acknowledged what she couldn't control and put together a clear path forward based on what was in her power. Ultimately, New Zealand had some of the lowest death rates from the virus in the world and her leadership stood the test of another election in 2020.

Ardern herself is clear that you don't have to choose between kindness and strength: kind *is* strong. She said, 'I think one of the sad things that I've seen in political leadership is – because we've placed over time so much emphasis on notions of assertiveness and strength – that we probably have assumed that it means you can't have those other qualities of kindness and empathy. And yet, when you think about all the big challenges that we face in the world, that's probably the quality we need the most. We need our leaders to be able to empathize with the circumstances of others, to empathize with the next generation that we're making decisions on behalf of. And if we focus only on being seen to be the strongest, most powerful person in the room, then I think we lose what we're meant to be here for. So I'm proudly focused on empathy because you can be both empathetic and strong.'[13]

Myth Three: 'There are kind people and unkind people'

The final myth is the 'Do-gooder Myth': the idea that some people are naturally kind all the time, while others are just not. It's the idea that the world is full of kind people and unkind people, and there's not much we can do about it.

We are all guilty of a certain level of passivity when it comes to how we think about kindness. You may have been reading about Steve Jobs and Elizabeth Holmes earlier and thought, 'Well, I'm not a business bastard, so I'm OK', or been thinking about the people in your life who you admire for their consistent and brilliant kindness. We all love simple narratives. However, the truth is a bit more complicated. I'm sure you can think back to moments in your life when you weren't kind – and some of them recently. I certainly can.

No one gets to claim 'kind' as part of their identity. We are only as kind (or not) as our last act. It helps to see kindness not as a noun, but as a verb.

Kindness is a Verb, Not a Noun

Kindness is action, not identity. We can't think of someone simply as being a 'kind person' or an 'unkind person'. We can't always guarantee that we ourselves will be kind, either – all of us will likely miss the mark from time to time. We can merely say that we believe in the power of kindness at work and that as far as possible within our powers, we will do kind things. And the beautiful thing about kindness being a verb and not a noun is that it's never about what we did or didn't do in the past, but all about what we can do, right now. Social media would have us believe otherwise, but it's not enough to use the right hashtags or say you believe in kindness: it's about action.

Hashtag Kindness and the Problem with 'Kindness as Identity'

Social media is full of people expressing their identity. I am always a little wary when I see hashtags like #bekind, yet just a day or so later you might find the same person being particularly unkind to someone else in the comments. In Part Three (Principle Six: Treat People the Way THEY Want to be Treated), *see also* page 155, we will talk about the problem with 'performative kindness' – for example, filming yourself giving money to a homeless person (largely because you think it might play well for 'likes'). Kindness is about the meeting of your empathy and positive intent (as coach Christina Kisley says, being *'for'* someone), with concrete action:

Kind = (empathy + positive intent) + action

We must all be careful to centre our kindness on others and be humble enough not to make ourselves the story (yes, think how I feel writing this book). Social media's focus is on 'our identity' rather than encouraging us to take selfless action and a lot of this is simply repeating insincere clichés. For example, so much of the social media discussion on kindness seems to centre around the idea of paying forward someone else's car-parking meter, yet putting coins in parking meters hasn't really been a thing for a long time.

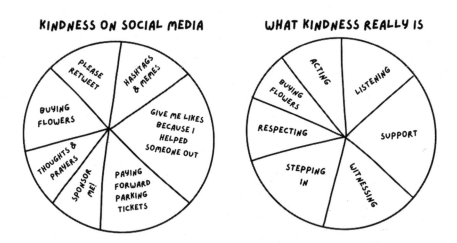

You'll notice that when we talk about what kindness really is, there's always a word that ends in 'ing'. Kindness is about doing. Without a verb, we run the risk of getting stuck on ourselves – stuck on the idea of kindness being part of our identity – rather than being focused on action.

Kindness is the Action That Happens in the Gap

In the moment just before any act of kindness, you see 'the gap'. The gap between someone else's needs and their happiness. The gap between what you could do and what's happening. The gap between thinking about making someone's day and actually making someone's day.

That's the gap.

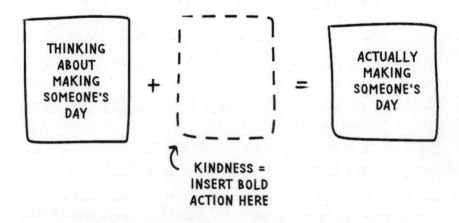

THINKING ABOUT MAKING SOMEONE'S DAY **+** = ACTUALLY MAKING SOMEONE'S DAY

KINDNESS = INSERT BOLD ACTION HERE

Bridging the gap, with kindness, is sometimes the easiest thing in the world. And yet other times, it can feel like a massive personal risk:

- 'What if they don't like what I'm offering?'
- 'What if I'm seen as being patronizing?'
- 'What if I miss the mark?'
- 'I'm not sure I have the time.'
- 'I've got my own problems.'
- 'I feel awkward.'
- 'There are other people who could step in and they'd probably do a better job.'

We panic and find a million reasons *not* to bridge the gap. 'What if?' this and 'what if?' that. But what if your self-talk was all wrong and you *did* make someone's day? What if your kind intentions were appreciated and loved? Then, you've created incredible human connection and perhaps pushed yourself out of your comfort zone too.

Not taking action is almost always the easier option but when we turn down the opportunity to be kind, we leave a lot on the table. We deny not only that person in need from being a potential receiver, but also, remember, the witnesses, the potential ripple effects that it creates and on and on.

Kindfulness – The Awareness of the Power of Kindness

Being Kindful starts with learning to spot 'the gap' more often and learning to relish it instead of fearing it. And then it is also about how we can create those ripple effects for others by helping to *create* the gaps, through our leadership and teamwork – giving other people permission to jump into more opportunities to be kind.

To be Kindful means to look at everything we do through the lens of kindness: 'How can I make this situation kinder?', 'How can I encourage others to be kind?', 'How can our culture at work make acting with kindness easier for everyone?'. I started this book by talking about my son, Roscoe, and how he is such a 'vessel for kindness'. Both through his own kind actions inspiring people and also the fact that he often needs a little bit of extra help, he inspires kindness in both friends and strangers.

As team-members and leaders, we can create the 'vessels for kindness' too: whether it's organizing a card for someone who's had a stressful time, or suggesting we set aside a few minutes of a meeting to saying something we appreciate about the person next to us, or by creating a 'kindness to customers' challenge like Ole Kassow did in his bakery (*see also* page 30), we all have the power to inspire others. We can point out 'the gaps' that we can all jump into with our actions and we can also *create* gaps for other people to jump into. We all want to be kinder, but often it helps when someone has created that vessel to make it easy – think about how often you tip in a café because someone put a tips jar there, or donate to a charity because someone you know is running a marathon for that cause. Usually we jump enthusiastically into 'the gap' at the slightest suggestion or excuse – kindness thrives when someone just creates that space and makes it easier to do than not.

This is the essence of Kindfulness. It goes beyond our own kind actions and becomes an ongoing way that we can look at the world: 'what can I create here, to make kindness as easy as possible for those around me?', 'what can I do to show the way?', 'what would this meeting or email or project look like if it was kinder?', and so on.

Kindful Practice

Kindfulness is a practice, much like writing, yoga, running, mindfulness, creativity or gratitude are practices. The more we practice, the better we get. It's got nothing to do with what we're born with – no one is magically a 'kind person', just as no one is born an Olympic gold medal athlete. It's all about our commitment to the practice and our belief that we can (and will) continuously improve if we commit.

Practice doesn't mean perfect. Sometimes we will get it wrong, just like a writer will sometimes spend a morning writing something then decide to press delete and start again. The great writers are usually those that keep showing up, learning over time not to fear the blank page, or what the critics might think.

When we view Kindfulness as a practice, it can be a powerful tool for personal development. We improve our listening skills, our ability to negotiate, to communicate, to empathize and to think differently. The list goes on.

Later, in Part Three of this book, I will introduce you to the cornerstones of my own practice: The Eight Principles of Kindfulness at Work. You'll be surprised or relieved to learn that I'm not perfect at this stuff, either. I cringe when I look back at some of the ways I've handled situations without the kindness they required. But the good news, for all of us, is that we can keep practicing. And that by confronting what feels challenging, we improve over time, too.

Sometimes, when we see 'the gap' and it feels risky to act, it's like jumping between high-rise buildings. The first time you jump, it feels like life and death.

If you do so 100 times, it's so effortless and comfortable that you may even want to up the ante. And of course, over time, we learn that each day as we pass through life, there are so many moments when the gap presents itself. We get better at spotting the opportunities, as well as jumping with both feet. And we get better at helping and inspiring others to notice the gaps, too.

I invite you to commit to Kindfulness as an ongoing practice – to be open and ready to take action, even when it feels on the edge of your comfort zone. I promise if you do that, you'll be enriched by what follows. And the challenge that follows below is designed to give you a little push if you need it. Please don't skip it!

Questions for Reflection

- When you think of inspiring leaders, do you think of the 'business bastards' or those eschewing quiet kindness? What makes a hero? Who decides? And what influences these stories for you?
- When have you been guilty of choosing 'Nice' over 'Kind'? What could you have done differently?
- Think about a time when you were courageously kind: were you committed to the truth with grace? Did you leap into 'the gap'?
- Can you think about a time when you didn't act but wished later that you had done? What was the barrier for you?

Kindness Challenge

This week's challenge is simple yet profound. Over the next week, I want you to take the actions needed to be kind (just like last week), but with a particular emphasis on those moments when it's either scary or inconvenient.

Look for 'the gap' – the moments when your empathy and ideas confer to show you that there's an opportunity to take action. When you see the gap, try not to give yourself the option of doing nothing. Act. Override your fears or your scarcity mindset kicking in. And then notice what happens, for you and for them. Then, when you're in the swing of things, you'll probably start to think a bit bigger and you may notice some opportunities to create the 'vessels' for *other people* to be kinder, too. Be brave and see what kind acts you can inspire others to create, too.

Write down some thoughts:

- What scared you?
- Did anything bad or awkward happen? If so, what was the consequence?
- Which moments of kindness were effortless and easy?
- How can you create more 'vessels for kindness'?
- Did you talk to those around you about this challenge? What was the reaction?

PART THREE
THE EIGHT PRINCIPLES OF KINDFULNESS AT WORK

KINDNESS STARTS WITH YOU

SET CLEAR EXPECTATIONS

LISTEN DEEPLY

PEOPLE FIRST, WORK SECOND.

ALWAYS.

BE HUMBLE

TREAT PEOPLE THE WAY THEY WANT TO BE TREATED

'WHEN YOU LEAD, FIRST OF ALL
THEY LEARN YOU.

SO YOU'D BETTER LIKE WHAT IT
IS THEY'RE LEARNING.'

FIONA DAWE CBE, COACH, FACILITATOR AND
FORMER CHARITY CEO

Graham Allco

The Eight Principles of Kindfulness at Work

Here, in Part Three, I'm going to take you through the Eight Principles of Kindfulness at Work. For a few years now, I have been leading workshops and short courses on this topic. As I teach and facilitate, I learn too, picking up the experiences and perspectives of everyone who participates – from financial services to charities to health professionals to engineers. Some of the case studies, quotes and stories in this book are from household name entrepreneurs and businesses, but many others are from people I've worked with or interviewed for this book, operating at all levels of all kinds of organizations. There's no single way to do any of this stuff, but I hope the range of stories helps you find your own way.

The ordering of the principles is deliberate and designed to take you on a journey of self-enquiry. We are going to start at the beginning: 'Kindness Starts with You'. This first principle is one that many of us find extremely challenging. Most of us are actually wired to be much less generous to ourselves than to other people. Then, with ourselves in check, we can think more about how we interact with those we work with, or lead. Principle Two is about how we 'Set Clear Expectations' and create the right operating environment both for good behaviour and success. And Principle Three, 'Listen Deeply', is of course vital to make sure that our expectations and values are aligned with those around us and to check the progress of what we're trying to achieve.

The next three principles are all human-centred. 'People First, Work Second. Always.' has for many years been my constant mantra as a reminder that people are human beings as well as resources and that we need to honour the need for dignity and proper work–life balance – not simply because it's the right thing to do, but because it also builds a team ethic and loyalty that gets results. Principle Five is 'Be Humble' and it's there to remind us that however lofty our position, we are all here to serve others. Getting the best out of people often means getting out of the way of them. And finally, in this little trio, 'Treat People the Way THEY Want to be Treated', is a reminder that in order to be truly kind, we need to understand people and what makes them tick, tailoring our kind actions to match their version of kindness, not ours.

The final two principles are at the end for a reason: 'Slow Down' takes us back to basics. So much unkindness is caused by stress and speed. When we bring back that sense of abundance and allow ourselves and others to catch a breath once in a while, it becomes much easier for all of us to be kinder. And the final principle is the essence of Kindfulness. It's all about culture and how we can create 'the gaps' for others to jump into, creating a perpetuating ripple effect: 'It Doesn't End With You'. But we do have to start with YOU.

'SELF-CARE IS NOT SELFISH OR SELF-INDULGENT. WE CANNOT NURTURE OTHERS FROM A DRY WELL. WE NEED TO TAKE CARE OF OUR OWN NEEDS FIRST, SO THAT WE CAN GIVE FROM OUR SURPLUS OF ABUNDANCE. WHEN WE NURTURE OTHERS FROM A PLACE OF FULLNESS, WE FEEL RENEWED INSTEAD OF TAKEN ADVANTAGE OF.'

– Jennifer Louden, author of *The Woman's Comfort Book*

---

1. Kindness Starts With You

Kindness starts with you. It's uncomfortable to hear, isn't it? This part of the book is all about practising self-kindness. We will focus on three very important areas here: self-talk, self-acceptance and self-care. These very phrases can bring up all kinds of negative emotions, which we will address head-on, but underpinning this principle are two very simple ideas:

- When we are kind to ourselves, we are doing the ultimate role-modelling: we are showing the people we lead and those around us that it is OK for them to be kind (to themselves and to others).
- By working on our own self-talk, self-acceptance and self-care, we are also training ourselves to become kinder. Our self-kindness ripples out and makes us kinder to other people too.

Your actions set the tone

We all have a bigger influence than we realize and it's easy to forget the extent to which the actions of a small group of people *become* the culture. We have more power than we think to affect our environment, even when we are part of a much larger whole.

Think about how little it can take to destabilize things. It's often just one or two stressed-out leaders, and usually without intention, creating a culture of stress, fear, guilt and toxic behaviour. One senior leader in a large overseas development organization told me this story about her boss:

> 'There's a culture of over-work. This past year, my organization has grown very quickly but has also experienced massive budget cuts, so it's been a really challenging time. Our boss is new in the job ... He's tried to signal that well-being is important and we need to take care of ourselves and that there's flexibility, but at the same time, everyone from the team has felt so much pressure and they see him burning himself out, so he's not doing the self-kindness thing. And because I know he's working crazy hours and is at breaking point, I also feel like I need to step up and not bring problems to him, so all the stress ... everything ... just gets pushed down. A lot of us feel burnt out, isolated and not connected to the team.'

A lack of self-kindness creates knock-on effects, which spiral far beyond your own influence:

1 You deny others your kindness because you simply don't see the opportunities to be kind when you're stressed or busy.

2 You make it harder for everyone else to be kinder to themselves and to others by feeding a negative culture around you.

There's nothing honourable or heroic about running ourselves into the ground. Often I catch myself thinking of self-kindness as somehow indulgent or selfish and when I do, I try to remember that self-kindness is an act of love and care – and not just for me, it's for the people around me too. It's about saying 'this is what the world could and should be like, for everyone'.

It's time to acknowledge our own needs and stop denying ourselves what makes for a better world. And when it's put like that, it sounds like such a rational, no-brainer of a choice and yet so many people I've worked with really struggle with this. Let's look at some of the reasons why.

Why is self-kindness so hard?

It *sounds* so rational and simple, but it *feels* anything but. When I first started working with people on their productivity over a decade ago, I thought productivity was mainly about having cool label makers, zero inboxes, the right apps and good systems. What I learned very quickly through coaching people was that mindset, how we think and how we talk to ourselves are more important than any tool or technique.

The art of good self-talk

Over the years, I've worked with and interviewed some pretty remarkable people. Business owners, high-performing leaders and entrepreneurs, young people with incredible energy and potential, older people with quiet wisdom and painful experience, Olympic gold medalists, professional clowns, inspiring authors, community leaders changing the world, folk musicians telling stories … It's a long list. One of the questions I'm sometimes asked when I do keynote talks is whether I notice any patterns in how high-performing or 'A-type' people think. My honest is answer is 'not really … except that all humans are weird'.

I've coached people whose impressive level of drive, when we've boiled it down, came from a desire to do better than the kid at school who bullied them 20 years ago, or a desire to gain the approval of strangers to make up for a lack of parental approval. Equally, I've met people who calculated, at a young age, exactly what they wanted their life to resemble and worked diligently backwards with a laser-like focus.

The way we think about success, money, work and what constitutes a 'good life' is different for all of us. The only constant is that one way or another, we are all weird. Perhaps you, dare I suggest, are sometimes a bit irrational, or you can get stuck easily and you may miss the obvious path. Equally, maybe you can hook onto important details that others might miss, or see someone else's pain before they do, or see numbers as colours painting a picture. Our weirdness can be a blessing as well as a curse. And what I know for sure is that understanding our biases, hang-ups, geeky passions and emotional patterns is fundamental to a successful life (whatever you determine that to mean for you). And of course, by understanding the motivations of others, we can work out what weirdnesses we might share in common and what weirdnesses are different. Sometimes it pays to turn your weirdness volume up to 11, other times it's better to rein it all in.

'WE DON'T HAVE TO WAIT UNTIL WE ARE ON OUR DEATHBED TO REALIZE WHAT A WASTE OF OUR PRECIOUS LIVES IT IS TO CARRY THE BELIEF THAT SOMETHING IS WRONG WITH US.'

Tara Brach, Psychologist, Author and Proponent of Buddhist Meditation

---

THE LIZARD BRAIN AND OUR WEIRD SELF-TALK

The amygdala, or 'Lizard Brain', is the part of our brain that gives us our 'fight or flight' response. It is there to keep us safe. It screams loudly when we're standing at the edge of the pavement and see a car coming, and even gives us the instincts to protect our children from harm. In evolutionary terms, it's kept our species going pretty well. It's why we bristle when our kids are involved in a playground territory dispute with another child, or when we're in a meeting and everyone is going around the table saying their names and right before it's our turn to speak we're saying to ourselves, 'Don't screw up, don't screw up, don't screw up.'

Think of the Lizard Brain as the part of the brain that gives us our primal instincts. It tells us if we're hungry, or cold, or even horny; it senses danger. Also, in the era of the human species where most of us are lucky enough to be cushioned from regular mortal danger, it's really bad at working out what is actual mortal danger and what just feels like it.

WHAT ARE OUR LIZARD BRAINS ACTUALLY WORRIED ABOUT?

Our Lizard Brain, perhaps because of the vital role it has played in our evolution, is often the part of the brain that shouts the loudest in our ear. It has an eye on survival and the conditions that might lead to danger: being ridiculed and cast out by our tribe, being judged and demoted, loss of money leading to a lack of food, and so on. We know this part of our brain isn't the logical part, yet it somehow takes over, often leaving us panicking about the worst-case scenarios that we almost certainly know won't play out.

Understanding our own Lizard Brain and knowing how to calm it down helps us develop much kinder self-talk. Understanding that everyone else has an equally weird Lizard Brain shouting nonsense in their heads helps us to provide the reassurance and psychological safety that are needed for productivity and innovation.

FEAR AND GUILT

The following are all examples of highly irrational Lizard Brain instincts that might stop us from taking time for ourselves and making space for kindness:

FEAR-TALK

- 'I will look foolish.'
- 'I will look unreliable.'
- 'I can't let my team down.'
- 'We need to hit our targets.'
- 'If I lose this job, I'll never get another one.'

GUILT-TRIPS

- 'I'm not working as hard as they are.'
- 'But I'm so behind on everything.'
- 'I'm being paid all this money, I'd better earn it.'
- 'I'm wasting this chance.'
- 'I'm letting my boss/client/team/myself down.'

Scarcity mentality vs Abundance mentality

As we discussed earlier, we are taught to see all work as *The Hunger Games* in a suit and tie. That for me to win, you have to lose; that for me to be rich, you have to be poor; everything is dog eat dog and that being a bastard is the way to succeed. Of course, that's just a story. But what if there was a different story? What if we all, actually, had everything we needed?

Money is always just a story but when it comes to money and resources, a lot of our narratives about money are shaped at an early age. Economist Peter Koenig's work teaches us to ask ourselves questions about our relationship with money. I've been lucky enough to have some important conversations about money with brilliant coaches like Charles Davies and Tom Nixon, whose work identifies the common money narratives. These include:

Money is ... security
　　　　power
　　　　freedom
　　　　dirty/evil
　　　　success

Of course, none of these things are true. They are just the versions of the story that we've grown up with.

My own early money memories were painful. They included me having to lie to my friends because I didn't want them to know I was on free school meals, my dad was losing his job and worrying about whether we'd lose the house too, and the annual pain of shopping for football boots or trainers, knowing I could try on the Nikes but I'd always have to settle for the cheaper alternatives which fell apart weeks later (which I'm convinced is the main reason I never made it as a Premier League footballer).

As a result of these early memories, and without even realizing it, I built a strong 'scarcity and security' narrative. It means I've always worked hard (these biases have actually formed an important part of my drive and motivation). But over the years, I've found them difficult to shake off. Fundamentally, if you believe that you need more money to feel secure (or free or successful or anything else!), then that will always be true. As I've earned more and become financially secure, my brain has just moved the goalposts so that my scarcity narrative is still there and still feels true. The point isn't to try and hit the arbitrary moving target in your mind, it's to learn to feel secure without hitting it.

'KEEPING UP WITH THE JONESES: SPENDING MONEY YOU DON'T HAVE FOR THE THINGS YOU DON'T NEED, TO IMPRESS PEOPLE YOU DON'T LIKE.'

Walter Slezak, actor

Self-Acceptance

STATUS ANXIETY

Philosopher Alain de Botton's book, *Status Anxiety*,[1] talks about the difficult emotions of comparison: jealousy, regret, yearning and a constant sense of dissatisfaction. We tend to compare ourselves to the people most similar to ourselves. No one is jealous of the royal family, de Botton argues, because they're 'too weird', but we compare ourselves incessantly to those we went to school with, or live next door to. Our desire to collect the physical and cultural symbols of status, and the envy we feel when we observe others doing so, encourages our sense of competition. The Smiths frontman Morrissey famously sang that 'we hate it when our friends become successful' but of course, the only reason we feel jealous is the sense that we are in competition with them and their success equates to our own inadequacy or failure.

Just as with money, if you're lucky enough to rise up the ranks of an organization or develop a successful career, you just shift the target of comparison so that the standard gradually increases and you never quite feel like you're at the finish line. And in the same way, the secret to prioritizing self-care is dismantling the arbitrary and moving targets of 'I'll feel successful when...' and learning to feel successful with or without the fool's gold.

When most of our Lizard Brains spend so much time in panic mode and we're surrounded by media messaging that reinforces a scarcity narrative, it's no wonder that feeling abundant is not the norm. A sense of abundance should not be confused with having won the lottery or attaining huge personal wealth (a study of millionaires and billionaires found that their definition of 'enough' changed as they grew wealthier and was, at any level of wealth, two to three times their current wealth):[2] what matters is that we see our current situation as abundant, not that we fix the idea of abundance to some moving goal that's always just out of reach.

Exercise: Abundance

Stop what you're doing. Pause and reflect on the two sentences below. Write them down. Say them out loud. Notice how it feels in your body and what feelings come up for you as you say these words:

- 'I am enough.'
- 'There is enough.'

Overcoming Self-criticism & Self-doubt

We are often our own harshest critic, too. We forget that other people have struggles. We compare our messy insides to everyone else's glossy outsides. Negative self-talk usually doesn't come from the logical parts of our brain, but it feels logical. According to clinical psychologist Nick Wignall, there are ten types of 'cognitive distortions'[3] that we should look out for, all of which can lower our self-esteem and cause anxiety. These are:

- **Mind-reading:** Assuming we can read someone's mind without actually having any evidence for it ('I've upset them', 'they look so bored', and so on).
- **Over-generalization:** Inventing negative patterns that don't exist, or just exaggerating a situation ('this ALWAYS happens to me', or 'I'm never going to make this work').
- **Magnification:** Taking one genuine flaw and making it bigger ('I forgot his name so now he's going to think I hate him').
- **Minimization:** Being dismissive of our own achievements or strengths ('the event was OK, but I forgot the cocktail sausages', or 'I know I'm good at this, but it isn't hard').

- **Emotional Reasoning:** Making decisions based on how we feel rather than what we value ('I don't feel like working on my book today').
- **Black and White Thinking:** Putting things into extreme opposite categories rather than seeing any nuance ('I'm such a failure but they seem to be such a success').
- **Personalization:** Taking more responsibility than we should for things that are outside of our control ('They screwed up, but if only I'd have coached them better').
- **Fortune Telling:** Predicting the future with our feelings ('I feel sure they're going to hate our proposal').
- **Labelling:** Taking one event and creating a permanent truth ('I'm such a bad presenter' after one presentation that didn't go well, for example).
- **'Should' statements:** Attempting to motivate ourselves, but with a guilt-ridden or negative statement ('I should work harder if I really want this promotion', or 'I shouldn't be so careless').

Exercise: Self-talk and Self-acceptance

First, with a pen and paper, write down the worst things you think about yourself. Take a few minutes. Write down the things that immediately spring to mind and also, scan back through your diary and think about times over the last week when your negative self-talk may have been in full swing. What were you saying to yourself in those moments? Write them all down.

Now, go through what you've written down and think about these questions:

- Is there any evidence that this is true?
- Does it fit into one of the ten 'cognitive distortions' above?
- Can you make an argument for the opposite to what you've written down being true? What evidence can you think of for that?

Finally, it's time to redress the balance with some positive self-talk. Choose some of these sentences or phrases and write them down, as many times as you like. Say them out loud. Keep writing them down or saying them aloud until you start to feel the truth of the statement. Here are some to choose from:

I am skilled.

I am good at _____.

I am loved.

I know that _____ loves me dearly.

I am doing well.

I can be grateful for the achievement of _____.

I am enough.

I have everything I need.

I am a success.

I am proud of _____.

There is so much to be thankful for.

Self-care

Turning around our negative self-talk opens us up to be kinder and helps us spot the opportunities to be kind that are all around us but the real role-modelling happens when people notice us prioritizing self-care. The phrase 'self-care' is one that many of us find difficult, again primarily because of our Lizard Brain's penchant for fear and guilt. Often we think of self-care – doing anything that primarily focuses on our own well-being – as somehow indulgent. In fact, it's wholly necessary if we are to maintain good mental health, good work–life balance and the empathy and sense of abundance that kindness requires.

The Busy-ness Fallacy

One of the reasons we don't prioritize self-care is that we think we're too busy. We say things like:

'I'll give myself a break when …'

- 'I hit this next deadline.'
- 'When we're through the restructure.'
- 'In the New Year.'
- 'In two weeks when it all calms down.'

Have you ever noticed how happiness and serenity are always just two short weeks away? Everything is going to calm down and you'll have acres of clear space in your calendar to start going to the gym again, or start eating healthier food?

This is the fallacy of busy-ness. When we're in the middle of a busy period, especially when we're running on adrenaline and working towards something that feels important, it can feel impossible to take a step back, give ourselves a break and recalibrate. Yet, of course, this is when we most need a little bit of self-kindness.

'Busy' has almost nothing to do with your workload: it's a state of mind. Again, once we dismantle the narratives in our mind that prevent this, we can make the time and space for self-care. And if it genuinely feels like there just aren't enough hours in the day, then you need to make some space. You need to start practising the art of saying no.

Exercise: Saying No

Self-kindness doesn't magically appear in our lives, we have to make space for it. And making space means saying no. Derek Sivers, the founder of CD Baby, has a lovely mantra about this: 'Hell yeah! or No'. Most of us need to practise saying no much more regularly than we do. Here are some different things to say no to:

- Meetings that you don't need to be in
- Requests from your team that someone else can handle
- Social events that don't excite you
- Your own expectations and unnecessary pressures you put on yourself

- Things you've already written on your to-do list but realize don't need doing or aren't a priority
- Requests from family or friends – you should be able to say no and have boundaries when you need some time for yourself
- Things that don't fill you with joy.

The Canaries in the Coal Mine: Five Warning Signs You Need to Be Kinder to Yourself

Often when we're busy, we neglect self-care. Perhaps it hasn't been something you've personally prioritized for a few weeks. If that's the case, then make sure you are regularly on the look-out for some of the warning signs that you're not being kind enough to yourself:

1 When was the last time you did something kind for someone else? Was it today? If you're struggling to remember, then that's probably a sign that your kindness with others has taken a hit because you're not being kind enough to yourself. You need to start with you.

2 Do you constantly hear yourself referring to mythical times ahead, where time, calm and space are plentiful? Hint: those times never arrive. Be kind to yourself now.

3 Are you regularly feeling tired, stressed or low? Give yourself what you need for a reset.

4 Do you find yourself snapping at others?

5 Are small things are becoming big things (you're more irritated than usual by stressful emails, confused by online purchases, or fuming when you're stuck in traffic)?

Whether we're comfortable about it or not, kindness starts with us. When we put on our own oxygen mask first – by transforming our self-talk and making the time for self-kindness – we are able to be kinder and more abundant in the way we think about not just ourselves, but the world. The challenge at the end of this piece is all about Random Acts of Self-Kindness. You may feel an aversion to taking up the challenge, perhaps in a way that you didn't over the previous two weeks. But I urge you to commit fully to the challenge. I promise it's not indulgent – and you'll be surprised at what you learn.

Questions for Reflection

- What are the unhelpful stories you tell yourself? How could you reverse these?
- How can you be a better role-model for others when it comes to self-kindness?
- In an ideal month, what activities would you have done to practise self-kindness? And how can you make sure every month gets closer to this ideal goal?

Kindness Challenge: Random Acts of Self-kindness

This week's challenge is going to sound easy, but it might be the opposite. Your challenge is to take some time for yourself – time that you don't think you can afford to lose – with no agenda other than self-kindness. It's up to you what this will look like and I'd prefer you to come up with your own thing, but since you're busy, here are some ideas that you can use as inspiration:

1 Go through your calendar and renegotiate things. Cancel some meetings and replace them with clear space.

2 Write a 'have-done' list of all you've achieved this week (at Think Productive we call this the 'ta-da' list). Spend some time giving yourself some credit.

3 Prioritize your sleep – cancel some plans and go to bed ridiculously early, or stay in bed until lunchtime.

4 Book tickets for a trip that's months away, so you have something to look forward to.

5 Go for a walk – it's never the wrong thing to do.

6 Have the cake.

7 Write down the things that bring you joy and value. Now, look at your bank statement. Notice the things you love that aren't reflected there and make a plan to spend money on what you love.

8 Spend an hour doing nothing (no phone. Nothing!).

9 What's your favourite spot in town? Drop everything right now and go there.

10 Who haven't you spoken to in a while? Call them.

KINDNESS
HERO

KINDNESS HERO: CASE STUDY
DENISE NURSE, CO-FOUNDER OF THE BLACK
FOUNDERS HUB – COMBINING AMBITION AND SELF-KINDNESS

Denise Nurse is a high-achiever: a lawyer, TV presenter and entrepreneur. Her early career was in corporate law before she set up her own firm, Halebury, with a friend in 2007, which they successfully sold in 2020. While working for BSkyB as a lawyer, Denise answered an advertisement for an internal competition at the TV channel and became a weather presenter, later graduating to present shows like BBC's *Escape to the Country* and the consumer affairs show, *Watchdog*. Recently, she's been working as the co-founder of the Black Founders Hub, a peer network supporting black people running professional services firms to help them grow their businesses.

Denise is clearly ambitious and driven, but one of the things that makes her such a great Kindful case study is how self-aware she is: 'In terms of managing all of it, I would say managing my brain has been the number-one thing I've had to do and had to learn. From very early on, I have worked with coaches and joined networks, so that I'm setting aside time to work on the bigger picture of what I'm doing, and not getting too sucked into all of the details because the details will keep coming in. There'll always be more. You have to set aside that clear time to think, "What am I doing?", "Why am I doing this?", "What's the bigger strategy?", "How can I look at my thinking to make that more effective?" It's a practice that I keep.'

Denise is a great example of someone whose kindness starts with her. She sets the example of asking herself the right questions and being aware of her own self-talk so that she can help other people going through the same things: 'Great leaders who practice the art of being kind to themselves have the ability to be kind to others. If you are running yourself to the ground, if you are not saying very nice things to yourself, if you are being your own worst enemy, it's hard to offer kindness to others truly, because it will come from a not-good place. Leaders who are able to do that are the ones who show true kindness.

'And listening. What's truly kind is to allow people to be heard, in whichever way they show up. It requires bravery to do that, but it's kind. And then to take into consideration someone else's viewpoint, even when it's uncomfortable and you don't like it, you have to examine that. You have to have real agency of your own mind and your own thoughts: to be able to sit with your own thoughts, examine that and then work out what it means for your organization.'

Denise has had a stellar career, but is self-aware enough to know that unless she takes the time to pause, step back and be kind to herself, then she's at the risk of burnout. Sustainable performance is only possible when we know our own limitations. We have to look after ourselves for the long haul. That's why kindness starts with you.

'CLEAR IS KIND, UNCLEAR IS UNKIND.'

BRENÉ BROWN, *DARE TO LEAD*

Graham Allcott

2. Set Clear Expectations

Setting clear expectations is the difference between a 'kind' working culture and a 'nice' one. There will always be times when someone or something doesn't quite hit the mark and we can only deal with them kindly if there's a shared understanding of what's lacking and how to fix it.

Great leaders bring clarity. They offer a clear set of boundaries and expectations, and hold their teams to consistent account. Being clear is an act of kindness in itself because it drives psychological safety – once people feel clear and comfortable in what they are doing, they are more able to express themselves and participate more fully in discussions of performance. The same is true of how we work with colleagues or managing up – bringing clarity to a situation puts people at ease.

Here, we are going to look at what I call the Framework of Expectation: the three Vs that set the bar and set the tone. Then, we'll look at how to make that expectation more human, real and specific, through personal mantras, as well as some other tools and practices that drive clarity.

The Framework of Expectation

When we think about leaders setting strategy, or anyone wanting to get clarity in their work, we can reduce what is needed down to some fundamentals. We need to be clear what our goal is (the 'why'), the way we're going to do things (the 'how') and how we are going to measure success (the 'what'). Even the most complex of business strategies must have these three components at their core. I call this the Framework of Expectation and it's easy to remember: three Vs:

- **Vision** – The big thing we're trying to achieve together.
- **Values** – How we're going to work together and what matters to our culture.
- **Value** – What success would look like (giving every single person a clear answer to the question of 'how do I bring measurable value to contribute to this team?').

VISION

'Why are you working so late?', President John F. Kennedy famously asked a cleaner on a visit to the NASA Space Centre in 1962. 'Well, Mister President, I'm helping to put a man on the moon,' came the reply. This legendary moment illustrates the power of having purpose in your work. Purpose is a great motivator and it's also something that, in the best companies, shines through into the product itself too. As Simon Sinek says in his TED Talk, *Start with Why*, consumers don't buy what you do, they buy why you do it. Whether you're working as part of a huge corporation, in a start-up, for a government or not-for-profit organization or just working for yourself, a compelling vision of what you are working towards is one of the greatest assets you have.

Great vision statements are the 'North Star' for an organization. Amazon's vision is 'to be earth's most customer-centric company, where customers can find, or discover anything they might want to buy online'. Oxfam's vision is 'a just world without poverty', while Tesla's is 'to accelerate the world's transition to sustainable energy'. For a long time, Nike's was 'Crush Adidas'. The idea is that whenever you're stuck in a meeting, or unsure about which projects to prioritize, these simple statements orientate you towards the right decision.

VALUES

Where vision gives us the 'why' of an organization, values provide the 'how'. Let's say your company's vision is to be number one in its field. Is that the only consideration when making decisions, or is it also important to you, collectively, to be known not only as great champions, but as sporting ones too? Are there some ethical considerations, or behaviours that are off-limits, in working towards your goals?

Values also shape the personality and culture of an organization. Google's company values are wrapped up in a document called 'Ten things we know to be true'. These include 'It's best to do one thing really, really well', 'You can make money without doing evil' and 'There's always more information out there'. These mantras are all based on Google's experience of building their organization and help to ensure that future employees continue to learn from what came before them and operate in a similar way. They confidently articulate what makes Google different and what has made it a success.

We can also use values to reinforce the right kinds of behaviour, too. Jonathan Austin is the founder and CEO of Best Companies, the organization that benchmarks which companies have the practices and cultures that make them the best to work for. He told me: 'So many people have brand values, but they don't describe the behaviour they're looking for within colleagues. So "Respect, integrity, communication and excellence" were the values of Enron. The interpretation of those values was obviously somewhat skewed. But if you describe the behaviour that you're looking for and definitely what you're not looking for, that gives people a framework ahead of joining that organization of what is expected for them.' So, if vision is the North Star, values are the compass. They help us to navigate problems with a greater sense of who we are and how we should be.

VALUE

These first two components, the vision and the values, are memorable mainly for their emotional pull. How will we know when the mission is complete or if we are acting in line with our values? We'll *feel* it. But for this next part of the framework, it's all about the cold, hard facts. What value are you expected to add? What's the target? What are the Key Performance Indicators (KPIs)? The job of leaders is about setting, negotiating and agreeing, for each person, the role they'll play in working towards the vision. So, the cleaner at NASA will presumably have been given a cleaning schedule every day, just as a salesperson is given a target to hit each quarter. Whether we're the CEO or the cleaner, knowing the role that each person plays in the mission brings clarity and better teamwork.

Great organizations operate with both values and value in play: they focus on results and pushing things forward as well as on doing things the right way. The most obvious 'value' for any corporate organization is 'profit' (and this is also vital for charities and the public sector in the longer term too), but of course there are many other ways to define performance, depending on the type of organization and the type of role. Here are just a few:

- number of people helped
- number of projects completed
- hours billed to clients
- changes created for customers/clients/audience
- growth in market share or customer acquisition
- number of sales enquiries generated.

In *Mastering the Rockefeller Habits*,[1] entrepreneur Verne Harnish talks about the key characteristics that set high-growth companies apart and one of them is having a tight grip on a small number of key metrics. Daily, rigorous focus on the things that matter most to your organization helps maintain focus and drives high performance. And although it may involve an uncomfortable conversation, or with some roles quite hard to pin down and define as a simple number, it's an important discipline. Defining and measuring the value you expect each member of the team to contribute also helps bridge the gap that can often exist between lofty plans and the fuzzy, messy reality.

How to Make Vision, Values and Value Real for Your Team

Defining the three Vs – our Vision, Values and Value – is vital for success, but it is often poorly implemented. It's easy to see why, too. These statements are often decades-old and the reality for your organization might have changed. They are, whenever they're written, a snapshot in time and the world changes around you. And of course, in larger organizations, it's a tricky challenge to articulate something that feels specific enough to focus on everybody and drive performance, but at the same time general enough that it can apply to everybody and everything.

PERSONAL MANTRAS

Often the best leaders I see are those that don't care if the company's vision statement feels a bit pie-in-the-sky, vague or outdated: they simply create their *own* framework of expectation that's still consistent with the wider operating environment, but crucially, is much more relatable and inspiring. If you manage people, think about creating your own, internal, team-wide mission, about how your team or department relates to the wider organization, or regularly sharing a personal mantra that describes simply your expectations of those around you. And the same is true if you're not in a leadership position – setting out the expectations or values that are important to you and how you work can be a shortcut to great communication.

A personal mantra is a short phrase that can be remembered clearly so that it's known and regularly repeated by the team, but that articulates a clarity of expectation. Timpson is one of the UK's most successful retailers and also a business that places kindness at its core (you'll hear more about them later in the book). Their motto for staff is 'Look smart and put the money in the till'.

It's a humorous way of getting across to employees the idea that as long as they have high standards of customer care, and are acting with honesty, then nothing else matters (Timpson has no marketing department and employs a very 'hands-off', non-didactic approach to how it manages its retail stores). At Zappos, founder Tony Hsieh's mantra was 'Be Adventurous, Creative and Open Minded'.[2] This simple phrase set the tone for so much of Hsieh's people-centred approach.

Here are some other examples of personal mantras:

'Work smart, break hard, leave on time' – this one was introduced to Think Productive by Elena Kerrigan, our MD. It articulates beautifully two things that we care passionately about and that orientate our decisions: we want to work in a way that is 'serious' and focused, but not for its own sake, but because doing so gives us the freedom to have a good life outside of work.

'To NOT consult is an insult' – Laura Woodcock is a project manager in one of the UK's biggest charities. She told me: 'I've introduced this as my mantra with my team. It's a reminder that if we want to do a project initiation document, we need to think about all the people that we've got to consult first, or else later it's going to feel to them like we are insulting them.'

'Fewer cakes, more cherries' – In one of the teams I ran, I worked with someone who was full of enthusiasm for starting new projects, but lacked the enthusiasm to follow through or actually manage or finish the things they'd started. One day I said to them that they should stop trying to make cakes and concentrate on putting the icing and cherries on the ones they'd already made, so that people could eat them. They wrote a version of this on a Post-it note and stuck it on their desk. Over time, the shorthand 'fewer cakes, more cherries' came to mean something powerful to the whole team: 'let's avoid the temptations of the shiny new initiatives and double down on what we're committed to'.

'Will this make the boat go faster?' – Ben Hunt-Davis was an Olympic gold medal-winning rower for Great Britain. He puts the team's success down to what they decided to do every day, not how they performed on the day. The simple question he asked himself at every point in the day was, 'will it make the boat go faster?'. That meant he said 'yes' to getting on the rowing machine because that allowed him to improve his conditioning and 'no' to the idea of going to the pub because that would have the opposite effect. Every decision was driven by whether it would affect this singular goal. I've seen this mantra adopted well in a couple of client teams as a way of eliminating unnecessary distractions and making sure enough focus was on pushing hard towards the achievements that really matter.

'People first, work second. Always' has been my personal mantra for many years. You'll hear a lot more about it later.

'I don't care if you screw up, as long as you own up and clear up' – I have heard various versions of this phrase over the years (some with added swear words), but it's such a powerful message: take ownership and try things, and don't pretend that mistakes aren't often an important part of the process.

Mantras add clarity, and clarity is almost always kind.

TEAM MISSION STATEMENTS

Greer Rios has taken the idea of a personal mantra to the next level, and created an entire mission statement just for her team. She is the Associate Vice President at MedArrive, a medical supply chain company based in Texas, USA. Greer attended one of my Kindfulness at Work programmes in 2021 and wanted to find a way to build some of the principles into her team. She created and shared an internal mission statement for her team – 'to be the kindest and most comprehensive procurement team'. This simple statement encouraged the team to interrogate how they'd instil kindness in their work and inspired many conversations that have helped shape the culture of the team. For Greer, there was an added layer of vulnerability to focusing on kindness with her team:

'Outside of work I'm a standup comedian too and despite being a leader and being professional in my work, I'm still known as someone who'll provide the snarky comment or crack the joke that others would think unsayable. I'd recognized that this mission statement was an opportunity for me to say to my team, "look, I'm planning to change a bit of me here and operate differently" and the mission statement held me accountable in achieving this.'

'FOR AN ORGANIZATION TO BE STRONG, YOU SHOULDN'T JUST BE LOOKING AT THE LEADERS AT THE TOP – YOU HAVE TO HAVE LEADERSHIP FLOWING ALL THE WAY THROUGH THE ORGANIZATION. A LEADER CAN SET THEIR OWN "LEADERSHIP TONE" FOR THEIR ACTIONS. AND THEN IT'S WHAT YOU DO TO DRIVE THAT WAY OF BEING, IN YOUR DAY-TO-DAY WORK.'

Rob Cade, Director, Capgemini

Exercise: Your Personal Mantras

What are the phrases that you find yourself repeating again and again to your team? Which of these best articulates the expectations you have for them? How could you make these better known among your team?

Spend a few minutes with a pen and paper, honing and crafting one or two perfect personal mantras (or even the first version of a team mission statement, which you could then consult with your team to develop further). Start a conversation about these mantras or mission statements with a trusted colleague so that you can road-test them for clarity.

At the same time, you might also like to email some of the members of your team: 'what are my catchphrases or mantras?', 'what do you see as the core values in the way I lead?', 'what do you think our vision is, and how do we know if we're successful (value)?' and so on.

Tools for Clarity

Once a framework of expectation is established, everyone's job becomes about alignment: making sure it is clear what's expected and driving performance towards the goals that have been set. This can be done in a number of different ways …

FIND THE POWER OF QUESTIONS

Questions force clarity. And questions should be everywhere: in your '1-2-1s' with direct reports, in meetings, in emails, on group chats and also in your solo thinking and planning time. I want to give one observation here about *how* to ask questions – because questions can also damage the sense of psychological safety that we are trying to provide for our team. And it's all in knowing when, and when not, to start them with 'why?'.

There are great times to ask 'why?'. When you set up a business or new project, 'why?' solves all kinds of problems – it can improve your product or service and it orientates you when you're lost. Knowing each other's 'whys' is crucial to the compromise and communication of every good relationship. Once you know someone's 'whys', it can be much easier to pre-empt or predict how they might think or act when new problems or opportunities show up. But, there are times when 'why?' is the obvious choice, but a bad one. 'Why did you make that decision?' or 'Why on EARTH did you do THAT?!' won't help you persuade someone to change course or reflect but may have the opposite effect – it'll make them double down to defend themselves.

'Why can't we do XYZ?' usually airs all the possibilities you don't want to hear and none of the ones that you do. For example, 'Why do you need me at this meeting?' ends with you going to the meeting you didn't think you should attend. And 'Why do you think you upset them?' puts the emphasis on the things that went wrong, not on the ways both parties could have done stuff better.

'Why?' questions, when they look forward, offer us infinite possibilities. Yet often when we are reflecting or analyzing, 'why?' has the opposite effect. It puts us on the defensive; it shuts down possibilities in favour of clinging to the precarious life raft of being right or saving face.

When you hear your brain jump to a 'why?', ask yourself if a 'how' question might be a better option. For example:

- How could that decision have been different? How else could it have been done?
- How could we improve on this or move on from this? How would this feel OK for them?
- How else could I contribute to the meeting outcome or project, given that we both know my time is squeezed?
- How could your behaviour or actions have been different? How would that have led to a better outcome?

If you want better answers, it pays to think hard about your questions. It pays to question with consideration. It's easy to rush in but the more effective method is to ask incisive questions, kindly, and give them the full space to answer.

L. David Marquet was a US submarine officer who, a few days before he was due to take command of the submarine he'd spent a year training for, found he was switched to a different vessel. Suddenly, he was inheriting a crew who all knew more about the new boat than he did. He stopped giving orders and started shifting the onus for decision-making onto his team, giving them the control over decision-making. As a result, he had to get a whole lot better at asking questions. In his book, *Leadership is Language*,[3] Marquet writes about unconscious language patterns we have inherited in the industrial revolution, and what we need to replace them with. One pattern is the asking of self-affirming questions. Self-affirming questions don't invoke curiosity, they merely seek to prove what we already know or want to be the case. For example:

- 'Does that make sense?'
- 'We're good, right?'
- 'Do you have everything you need?'
- 'Is it safe?'

These kinds of questions ultimately just serve to get people to go along with your instructions and view of the world. They don't seek data and the only option in response is reassurance. Instead, we can focus on more open-ended questions that seek an update rather than a close-down of data. These are questions like:

- 'How safe is it?'
- 'What are we missing?'
- 'What are the risks and probabilities of risk here?'
- 'What could have gone better?'
- 'On a scale of zero to five, how ready are we to launch the product?'

Starting questions with 'how' and 'what' are more likely to give you new data, whereas 'why' can be good to establish intent, but rarely helps as you progress. Self-affirming questions generally uphold the status quo.

WAVING THE FLAG FOR SPECIFICITY

One of the most important components of performance is specificity. What we need, and what our teams need, for every single thing we work on, is:

- A specific desired outcome
- The next physical action.

We need to know what the target is for value we are trying to create, in the most specific terms we can (for example, 'run a successful conference' is subjective, whereas 'run a conference that attracts 500+ paying delegates and brings in

£150K in sponsorship revenue' is a much more specific version of that same outcome). And then, we need to know what starting looks like. With anything creative (and most things are!), often the hardest part is staring at the blank page, or overcoming that feeling of being stuck to gain momentum. This is where the art of specificity comes in.

Encouraging people to focus discussions on the specifics is a thankless task, because it often means dwelling on a conversation that half the room thinks has already been resolved. But it's not resolved until it's clear. Specificity is important in defining problems, but it's even more vital when dealing with the nuts and bolts of team performance: 'what's the next physical action?' (the word 'physical' roots us in our bodies, helping the mind's eye to see whether we're emailing, or phoning, or mind-mapping or scouring Google). 'Who's doing what?' (and each action or area should have a SINGLE designated person, held accountable – that's not to say they have to do all the work themselves, but they're responsible for overseeing the progress and calling others in to make it happen). When is this due? (and it's best to always have a date – I ban the use of the word 'ongoing' in meeting notes, because it generally leads to inaction).

Matt Cowdroy, Director of Think Productive Australia, is nicknamed by his colleagues (and some clients) 'the King of Clarity'. After every meeting, he sends a simple email with a summary of the specific actions, who is leading on each one and any other important points to remember. He told me: 'I sometimes worry it can seem pedantic, but people always say they really appreciate it – far better than having those actions forgotten or misremembered in a couple of weeks.'

It is kind to insist on getting the specifics agreed and written down. Removing doubt and vagueness allows us all to work with facts, not judgement. That clarity is kind, because it helps everyone feel secure that they're working on the right things and reduces their fears, guilt and negative self-talk.

FREQUENCY & REPETITION

Peter Mandelson was one of the most important components of the New Labour project that won three consecutive General Elections for Tony Blair. One of Mandelson's most famous pieces of advice about communication was 'It is only when you're sick of hearing yourself repeat the same message over and over again that your audience is just beginning to get it'. It also makes it look easy: opening remarks at an event or in a meeting that remind people simply but clearly that the main thing is the main thing and then here's how what we're gathered here today to do fits into that main mission.

Such repetition can *feel* unnatural. Reminding people, when yes, some of them will already know the thing you're about to say, can seem patronizing. But this is an instinct that is good to override. Far better someone hear the important thing twice (and the second time they're likely still digesting its implications anyway) than a whole bunch of people miss the message.

Smaller and more frequent interventions are generally a better route to clarity than longer and staggered. Here are some examples:

- **Feedback, either for the whole team or for individuals:** Do it daily, not weekly.
- **Supervisions:** 45 minutes once a fortnight is better than an hour and a half once a month.
- **Team meetings:** A 15-minute daily 'huddle' is more focused and effective than an hour's team meeting at the start of the week.
- **Weekly welfare check-ins or project update reports on group Messenger apps** are better than monthly ones
- **Asking everyone the same question, every day:** 'What's our progress towards the key metrics, or the main goals?' might feel like overkill, but the discomfort it creates in all of you if there's no progress leads to exactly the right kinds of work being prioritized.

When you keep repeating the vision, values and value you're expecting people to create, you help reinforce the framework of expectation. In your own head it might sound like a broken record, but it means everyone else is humming the right tune.

ROLE-MODELLING

Trust is at the heart of every transaction and every high-performing team is bonded by high levels of trust and understanding. And there's one thing that erodes trust quicker than almost anything else: hypocrisy. We've all heard the disparaging saying 'Do as I say, not as I do' to describe managers who are seemingly unwilling to hold themselves to the same standards as they hold others. Perhaps the opposite of this saying is one I've heard from some inspiring leaders in moments of tougher love: 'Don't tell me, show me'.

Leading by actions as well as words is critical. When your own actions don't seem to prioritize the same things that your words do, then you create confusion in those around you: which version of you are they supposed to follow? There are a few ways that role-modelling can be used as a powerful tool for reinforcing clear expectations:

- Being the person who is vocal about saying no to things that are outside of the values, outside of the vision, or not obviously contributing value. This empowers others to follow your decisive lead.

- Being willing to have the truthful, difficult but kind conversations, instead of shirking the responsibility for them (being truly kind, avoiding the temptation to slip into 'nice').

- Visibly prioritizing your self-care (such as leaving on time, encouraging 'human' chat about lives outside of the office): remember that some people find self-kindness really tough. Show them the way.

- In meetings, allowing people the space to be curious, ask powerful questions and think critically about how things contribute to the framework of expectation.

- Being open about what you don't know, what you're struggling with, or what others have helped you with. Doing so sets a culture where people stop feeling like they need to be superheroes and/or feel the pressure to know everything and start seeing that collective wisdom and effort are better than any one individual.

- Discussing and celebrating mistakes. Again, it creates an expectation that mistakes are part of the process – sometimes even the vital part. This, in turn, boosts psychological safety as well as fostering innovation.

There are no special powers and shit happens. But also, great things happen when we lead from the front, especially when we do so with humility, honesty and human authenticity.

RITUAL

Life is full of rituals — from the big life moments like weddings and funerals to the smaller and simpler acts such as breaking bread with friends or shaking hands, rituals are our opportunity to make sense of things and establish a consensus of meaning. Rituals help a team to communicate and relate to each other personally, outside of the confines of tasks and projects, and you've probably worked in places where birthdays were celebrated with endless cakes, baby showers were held before someone went on maternity leave, or where everyone went out for a Christmas meal together. But more subtle rituals, based around the work itself, can help reinforce the framework of expectation as well as giving people a chance to express their gratitude, bask in some glory or bond with colleagues in new ways. Here are a few examples of rituals that all help reinforce expectations and increase communication:

- On a team call or group chat, ask each person to share their 'win of the week'.
- Ask each person around the table to say something they value about the person to their left.
- Award prizes or trophies for results or behaviours that align with the values.
- 'Spotlight on', where each week, a different person's work is highlighted and explained to the rest of the organization.
- On group chat, operate a 'Truth Tuesday', where everyone has a place, in safety, to share the less glamorous stuff, like 'this feels stuck' or 'I'm struggling with this'.
- Failure awards (because by making failure less scary, we increase innovation and encourage learning).

All of this creates the spaces and pedestals that allow others to thrive.

'CLEAR COMMUNICATION SETS EXPECTATIONS – THE LANGUAGE WE USE, ATTITUDES TO CONFLICT AND CONSTRUCTIVE FEEDBACK. WHENEVER WE ARE CLEAR WE REMOVE MISINTERPRETATION, BARRIERS TO DELIVERY AND NEGATIVITY.'

Teresa Hicks, Director of Strategic Partnerships,

The Raspberry Pi Foundation

ACCOUNTABILITY

A key tool in upholding trust, ensuring focus and driving performance is accountability. It works best where the value that someone is kept accountable for is negotiated and agreed rather than just imposed. It's also a really important component for organizations or cultures where the tendency is to shy away from the hard facts and numbers, focusing on 'nice' consensus rather than the discomfort that comes with stretching to achieve potential. And accountability works best when it's not just one-way: as a leader, facilitating the conversations within a group to allow each to be accountable to the collective is a powerful way to build trust and ensure that activity is focused on what matters most. As a leader, you should be comfortable both in holding your team accountable but also in allowing them to hold your leadership accountable too.

My experience is that accountability is best in short and frequent bursts – annual appraisals and annual planning meetings are great for lots of things, but generally the priorities and the operating context shifts so much in the space of a year that the goals chosen one January are not what you'd choose in June or September. A daily 'huddle' meeting with the team, setting everyone accountable for just one or two things, is far more effective than an annual session agreeing huge nefarious project plans. Working in an 'agile' way, where typically everyone on the team works towards a common goal in a period of two weeks or even less, we get an idea of the power of ongoing, short and frequent bursts of accountability. Generally, the closer in time the actions being delivered are to when they were discussed, the clearer and more specific the outcomes are. Time and foggy memories have a funny way of reducing clarity, which often leads to procrastination or breakdowns in communication.

And a monthly or fortnightly '1-2-1' meeting is a great focus point for accountability – starting each meeting by recapping the actions and targets from last month's meeting can be a great way to set a good rhythm each month, as well as providing an obvious, clear and non-awkward route into diffi-cult performance conversations. And if there are struggles at work or problems at home, having this kind of relaxed yet focused window of time in the diary is a kind way to bring such issues to the surface.

Kindful Feedback

Feedback is perhaps the most important tool for maintaining a constant conversation about whether performance and behaviour matches our framework of expectation. In his book, *The Practice*, Seth Godin[4] describes the creative process as being defined by the phrase 'Here. I made this'. It shows us that creating *anything* is an inherently vulnerable place to be. We are asking someone to react to our work, or give us their verdict on our perfor-mance. Asking for feedback, especially face to face, can be awkward and uncomfortable. It's easy to fear it, but over time, when we create the right kind of environment for this, it can become a whole lot easier. We just need ways to break the tension.

The word 'feedback', used in a work context, is a relatively recent thing. It was popularized after NASA used it to describe the regular 'feedback loop' between a space shuttle and mission control: 'Are we on track?', 'What's your current angle of trajectory?'. And depending on the answer, they'd know if the shuttle was on course to reach the moon, or needed to adjust.

Feedback is best served in this small, constant and consistent way rather than via one daunting annual appraisal. A culture of regular feedback means everyone is used to it and the less palatable parts are easier to digest. Here are a few observations about how to make feedback your super-power.

'IS THIS THE BIT WHERE I SLAP YOU ROUND THE FACE WITH A KIPPER?'

When I'm writing books, I always ask a selection of my peers to review the first draft before it goes to my editor, using focus groups. It's a stressful stage in the process of a book. The text often feels raw and incomplete, and I'm not fully happy with what I've done. Nevertheless, I've got months of work behind me and have yet to receive a single piece of feedback, so it's important to road-test.

I'm anxious to know whether people relate to what I'm writing, whether they think it's going to be useful, and of course what it needs to make it better. So, as you can imagine, it's a point in the process where I'm operating a lot from the Lizard Brain, with swirling emotions of fear often outweighing the logic. One of the first ever focus groups I ran included my friend Sean Sankey, a clever and thoughtful management consultant. We were a few minutes into the call and I'd explained the progress of the book so far and what kind of feedback I wanted; we were getting to the point where I was about to give Sean the spotlight so that he could run me through his feedback.

'So, is this the bit where I slap you round the face with a kipper?', he asked. We were doing this over the phone, but the tone in his voice still managed to reveal the playful glint in his eye. His question immediately broke any tension and that brief moment of understanding that this was all part of the process and wasn't a personal attack made the feedback he gave much easier for me to hear and for everyone else on the call to share their own feedback. A brilliant example of truth and grace.

Why Sean chose a kipper, I don't know. I suspect it comes from the classic Monty Python 'fish-slapping dance' sketch, where Michael Palin and John Cleese hit each other in the face with fish. You can use whatever metaphor you choose, but the important thing is to prepare the ground for the awkward part, making that moment psychologically safer for everyone.

'GIVE ME THE LAST 20 PER CENT'

I worked for a boss who would not only seek my feedback, but also actively encouraged me to be bold. He would often say, 'I want you to give me the last 20 per cent.' His idea was that people giving feedback usually give 80 per cent of the truth, but hold back that final 20 per cent, usually out of a fear that it might be awkward or hurt the person's feelings. By creating the expressed permission to be authentically honest, I was able to say the things that I might otherwise have held back. It was a powerful phrase that I often use myself in similar situations, reminding the people I'm working with that progress often comes from the discomfort we feel at the edges – that final 20 per cent is usually the most important part, and with a bit of skill, we can get to it kindly.

'Benevolent Critique'

Sarah Stein Greenberg heads up 'd.school', the design school at Stanford University. The culture at 'd.school' is incredibly people-centred and as you might expect, full of creative and surprising ways of working together that are designed to keep everyone's brains open to curiosity and finding the best ideas.

But of course, design isn't just about creative ideas, it's about finding the ideas that work when tested. This requires constant feedback and a high level of psychological safety, as doing creative work inherently means you open yourself up to regular subjective judgement. In Sarah's book, *Creative Ideas for Curious People*,[5] she talks about the idea of 'Benevolent Critique', a way of presenting feedback in as kind a way as possible. She told me:

'We want to be hard on the work, but soft on the people. And that is one place where kindness really manifests in our environment. It's like when you are critiquing student's work, or the work of your colleagues, or even your own, you want to separate the person from the work that they have produced. And you want to ask questions like, "what's the goal of this work?" Not like, "you know, well I really didn't like it when you decided to make it purple!" and more like "well, what are the goals of this work? And does being purple actually help it meet its goal?"

'By talking about it in the third person, rather than personalizing it, that is a really nice language approach, to be able to say, "we're focused on the quality of the work in whether it's serving its goal – not whether you are a good designer". That allows just enough distance to help you become a better designer, because you're taking the feedback and you're able to just slightly de-personalize it and make sure you can hear the critique, hear the feedback. And that, of course, then really makes that work more likely to succeed. It's kind, but there's also an underlying business reason for that kind of distinction too.'

Exercise: The 9 and the 1 – Feedback to reinforce

When asked for feedback, I can sometimes fall into the trap of gravitating to where my critical-thinking brain wants to go, rather than pausing to think, 'OK, this person has worked really hard on this and they want to hear kind words, reassurance or some recognition for their efforts'. It's led me to develop a bit of a rule for myself: 'The 9 and the 1'.

The idea is simple. For every one piece of feedback that's critical or negative, make sure there are nine bits of feedback that say 'love this!', 'spot on here', 'this is great and you could add this', and so on. If you're struggling to maintain the ratio, well it just means you need to go out of your way to make someone's day!

Try this exercise over the coming week, keeping a tally in the back of your notebook, or on your phone. Even on the days when you don't meet the ratio, it should at least skew your feedback in the right direction. Feedback should be something you drip-feed all day, every day and something you build into the culture, not something you drown someone with once a month.

Delivering Uncomfortable Feedback with Truth and Grace

This is all good in theory, but when you're face to face with someone and you need to deliver uncomfortable truths, it's hard. Sometimes it's helpful to have some structure for the discussion so that you have some steps to follow. This can sometimes help to put the issue on the table and have you both view it as if you're looking at a messy painting together, rather than be sat opposite the table from each other and it feel like a duel is about to take place.

When we give feedback, it should be delivered with truth and grace. The truth is important. It's the commitment to another person's growth and the commitment to making the work better. And grace matters, too. It's about being kind, recognizing that no one likes to receive bad news and knowing that as humans, we don't often fall short on purpose – there may be other things going on behind the scenes. Here's a very quick process for giving feedback with truth and grace, which I've used with people as part of my Kindfulness at Work programmes:

- **Step One (before you give feedback) – process your own thoughts first.** If you're annoyed with the person, don't try to give feedback yet. If you haven't gathered your words yet, wait. Hold tight and process your thoughts and emotions before you start.
- **Step Two – Situation.** Where did this thing happen? When? What's the wider context?
- **Step Three – Behaviour/Performance.** What specifically are we talking about? What did they do? What didn't they do? And so on.
- **Step Four – Impact.** Why does this matter? What happened that we particularly want to see again, or don't want to see again?
- **Step Five – Discuss.** Leave the space for them to process what they've heard, ask questions, think about what else might be going on here and so on.

BIFF

Behaviour, Impact, Feelings, Future (BIFF) is another simple process and is used a lot by police and other public services. This whole process is less of a discussion and more of a quick way to deliver feedback, so it should take no more than a few sentences and 20–30 seconds and then you allow for discussion once you've followed these four steps. If you were pulled over for speeding by a police officer, for example, they might use 'BIFF' like this:

- Behaviour – Our speed detection device just clocked you were doing well over 40mph in a 30mph-speed limit there.
- Impact – The research is that for every 10mph over the limit, there's a huge jump in fatalities.
- Feelings – Part of my job is visiting the victims' families to tell them about accidents and I really wouldn't want that for your family.
- Future – This time I'm going to leave that at a warning, but if it happens again I'd have to book you for that / I'm asking you to stick to the limit from now on.

BIFF is great for really quick interactions, but it can also be more flexible: for example, when you focus on feelings, you can open the discussion up to ask the other person for their feelings too and in the part centred on the future, you can also ask them to describe how they'll do things differently rather than have you prescribe it to them. In fact, sometimes BIFF is extended to BIFFO, where the 'O' stands for 'Open question'.

'BE HARD ON THE WORK, BUT SOFT ON THE PEOPLE.'

Sarah Stein Greenberg, Director, d.school, Stanford University

---

KINDNESS HERO: CASE STUDY
FIONA DAWE CBE, HUMAN-CENTRED KINDNESS

As chief executive of Youthnet, the UK charity sector's first tech startup, Fiona Dawe created a distinct culture that won them awards as 'best charity to work for'. Fiona's leadership style was influenced by the work of Nancy Kline and her pioneering 'Thinking Environment' framework, and now as a facilitator she is bringing this approach to organizations. She told me about how Youthnet became a 'Thinking Environment' and what that meant for the culture: 'We're human beings. And if we're treated well, we think better. And then we behave better. So, creating a compassionate, human-centred and kind culture is all about treating people well. With respect. When people feel psychologically safe, then (a) they behave better. And (b), they think better. So, you get a highly productive team and organization. That doesn't mean if you respect people that you love them or you even like them particularly, but you do respect them.'

The idea of 'treating people well' doesn't always mean they get what they want. It's not about being soft. In fact, it can be quite the opposite. In order for people to have trust in you, they also need to see consistency, fairness and a congruence between the values and behaviours that the leaders encourage and what happens on the ground

Fiona continues: 'I used to say to people "we don't have to treat people horribly". But you do have to be very rigorous. It's not fair, on everybody in the organization, if there's some people taking the mickey and getting away with it. Then everybody goes, "well, the leadership is shit". So that's the other side of being a kind leader. You have to, in my experience, absolutely call out anything that's not OK. You've got to have high standards. And if you say this matters, you have to make it matter.'

In charities, the culture can often veer more into 'nice' and neglect the truths that are truly 'kind'. Fiona's leadership added the clarity to ensure this didn't happen there: 'You actually create quite a challenging culture. I mean, Youthnet was not a coochie-coo place. It was really fun to be there and people felt very comfortable but we would say, "call things out!".

And we would call things out. I remember having wash-up meetings [to conclude a project] with partners and we would say, "oh well, that project, there were things that went really well. But this was a pile of rubbish. And that went to the rats, and so on". And people would think the world would fall in. But that was actually about getting it better. So, excellence isn't necessarily being nice. It's about being thoughtful and challenging, and it's very human-centred.'

Questions for Reflection

- What are your values?
- What are your organization's values?
- Which of these values are kind? Do any of them lead to unkindness?
- What behaviours or standards are important in how other people work with and interact with you?
- If you're a leader, where do you lack clarity in your leadership? What can you do differently?
- Who do you trust in your team to give you feedback about when you are clear and kind, and when you miss the mark?

Kindness Challenge: The Four Coins

Often we focus on feedback as a heavy thing to do when times are hard but actually, offering small but regular doses is a great way to reinforce the 'framework of expectation'. This week's challenge is designed to flex your Kindful feedback muscle and make it a regular practice.

Simply put four coins on the left of your desk, or in your left pocket. Each time you give someone feedback throughout the day, move a coin from the left-hand side to the right. The aim is that every day, you are moving all four coins from left to right, thereby volunteering at least four pieces of feedback each day. Doing so forms the habit for you and also forms the culture for those around you too, so you'll likely receive more feedback from colleagues on a more regular basis too. Kind, regular feedback is one of the keys to high-performing teams that deliver exceptional results.

'REAL LISTENING IS A WILLINGNESS TO LET THE OTHER PERSON CHANGE YOU. WHEN I'M WILLING TO LET THEM CHANGE ME, SOMETHING HAPPENS BETWEEN US THAT'S MORE INTERESTING THAN A PAIR OF DUELING MONOLOGUES.'

ALAN ALDA, ACTOR, SCREENWRITER AND DIRECTOR

Graham Allcott

3. Listen Deeply

'I think you'll have a good career, but there's something that I think you'd do well to learn that would make you even more successful. Can I tell you what it is?'

I had gone to visit Christopher Spence CBE. Spence was one of the most respected figures in the UK not-for-profit sector, the founder of the HIV/AIDS charity London Lighthouse and was now chief executive of Volunteering England. The walls of his office had pictures of him working with Princess Diana, Sir Elton John and a raft of leading politicians.

He was where I aspired to be and I was nervous about my first one-on-one meeting with him. I was the new young-punk CEO of Student Volunteering England, but what added to my nerves was that just two weeks before accepting that job, I'd been offered a job working directly for Christopher. I'd turned him down to take the riskier role that had a better job title and more opportunity for growth and autonomy if I got it right, but, clearly, I was starting this meeting on the back foot. We were about half an hour in and getting on very well, when he suddenly broke off to offer me his advice.

'I have huge admiration for you. I'd love any advice you can give me,' I replied.

'You don't look people in the eye enough. Take today. You're talking to me, but your eyes are all over the place. People need to know that you're paying them attention. They need to know you think they matter. They need to see you listening.'

As he said this, Christopher leaned forward and looked me deeply in the eyes, in a way that felt simultaneously terrifying and yet warm. He continued: 'As I'm talking to you right now, there is nothing else on my mind. I'm totally focused on this conversation. When you learn to do that, people will really listen to you.'

After the meeting, I felt like a whole new world had opened up. This strangely intimate moment taught me the importance of personal connection and the power of creating the space to make sure people felt heard. It remains to this day one of the most memorable and influential moments of my entire career.

One of the kindest things you can do for another human being is to listen deeply and wholeheartedly to what they have to say. We should be interested in what is being said, but also in the way it's said and what's *not* being said. Listening is a skill, rather than a behaviour. It needs to be sharpened, developed and practised regularly. Here, with the help of clinical psychologists and management best practices, we're going to focus on how to listen more deeply.

Paying Attention

It's often said that time is the most precious resource we have, when really the truth is slightly subtler than that. The most precious resource we have is our full attention. Attention is the fuel of deep relationships. Because it's so precious, when we give someone else the fullness of our attention – whether a life partner, an employee or a friend – it is extremely powerful.

The power of listening can bring about radical change: it can spark new ideas, change how we think about ourselves and each other, help someone overcome difficult emotions and build deep connections between us. People notice the quality of your listening. If you listen deeply, it's not only an opportunity to discover things and create change, but it's a chance to set the tone within your organization. Organizations that learn to listen are the ones that drive psychological safety and all of its associated benefits: clearer thinking, increased engagement, the ability to take calculated creative and strategic risks and higher productivity.

Deeper Listening

There's always more to listen to. The job of listening is never finished and a proactive approach creates the right conditions for deeper listening to take place, both for ourselves and to role-model that as something that everyone should seek to do, too.

Listening takes place in a variety of settings and on different scales, from the macro-scale of culture through the medium-scale of meetings and down to the intimacy of micro-scale one-on-one conversations. When was the last time you worked on your one-to-one listening skills? Since conversation is such an everyday activity, we don't tend to give it too much thought, but precisely because of how commonplace it is in our lives, and how critical good conversation and good listening is to the quality of relationships, it is one of the biggest improvement opportunities we each have.

We're going to focus first on preparing the ground for good conversation, then look at some insights and good practices that will help us be a kinder listener in a conversation. Of course, one of the difficulties we have as a listener is that sometimes we have to be in conversations that feel uncomfortable, so we'll finish up by looking at what to do when it's hard.

Preparing the Ground for Good Conversation

Listening and having a productive conversation is a choice – for both parties. We have to make a conscious decision to favour listening and to put curiosity above ignorance, convenience or just doing something else. Once we've made our choice to listen, we also need to do the preparation that a deep conversation requires.

HYPOTHESIZING

Before any one-to-one conversation, think through where the person might be coming from, the situation they find themselves in and how that might play out in the conversation. Psychologists talk about the idea of 'hypothesizing': spending some time putting themselves in the other person's shoes and imagining what stories they're telling themselves about this situation. How are they feeling? What do they think is going to happen in the conversation? What do they think of me? What else is happening in their lives?

Hypothesizing is an important component of empathy. It can help you to imagine how various factors play into people's experience of the conversation, such as gender, race, religion, age, class, education and sexuality. Thinking about how these factors might contribute to the likely perspectives and feelings of the person we are about to have a conversation with can be a useful tool in enhancing our empathetic listening skills.

In work, we hypothesize all the time. We'll think about how a certain piece of news might be received, what might happen if we put a particular person under more pressure, or what the intended or unintended consequences of a change might be. This thought process can be formalized and written down, or in certain circumstances you may have a supervision meeting with your line manager which becomes a natural place for hypothesizing about conversations that are coming up. But it can also simply be those passing thoughts as you're driving or out for a walk. Questions to ask yourself might be things like:

- How might meeting with me 'feel' to them?
- What else might they be bringing into the room with them? (Stress, disagreements, previous experiences and so on.)
- What do I think the difficult parts of this meeting might be? What might we both ask for?

EASING IN

The brain is a muscle and listening skills can be practiced and developed over time, but, like any muscle, we need to warm up before we jump into strenuous activity. Nancy Kline, author of *Time to Think*,[1] talks about the concept of 'arriving': the idea that people don't arrive when they sit down in the room, but when their mind is fully present on the person and topic at hand. It's almost as if they arrive twice. If someone arrives while quickly reading an email, or is flustered after dealing with an emergency, then it may take a few minutes to take their mind off what's just happened else-where – to fully arrive. We all know about the importance of building rapport and polite conversation before we get on to the main 'business', but this can be easily neglected. It is a useful (and kind) listening exercise in itself, to try to be aware of when someone has arrived for the second time.

TECH ETIQUETTE

Etiquette in face-to-face conversations matters too. Are we going to focus on laptops and phones here, or make the deliberate decision to put those away? Are there exceptions, or things for which we need to be 'on call'? Another good way to ease into a conversation and make sure both of you have your attention fully on each other is to start (after a little warming up) with a quick chat about tech etiquette.

TALKING ABOUT TALKING, BEFORE YOU TALK

Some people prefer Zoom or the phone, others might choose a walk in the woods where you don't make eye contact, or maybe it's an intimate coffee shop with a cake. Some like direct and honest communication, others like to know what's coming. Working out how someone likes to communicate can be as simple as asking them, much as at the beginning of a line management rela-tionship you might ask, 'What do you need from me as a colleague/manager?' or 'What bugs you about the way people manage you?'

If you don't feel confident in having these kinds of conversations with-out structure, then personality profiling tools such as DiSC or Myers-Briggs can be a great way to get people focused on discussing their own working styles and personal preferences, and provides a shared vocabulary and clear beginning, middle and end to the discussion that helps everyone feel safe.

Likewise, away days and more strategic conversations can be useful, given that they naturally create a dynamic that is removed from day-to-day work. Including some elements of reflection as well as a focus on what's needed in future means that old wounds can be healed and lessons learned for the future too.

BRINGING KINDNESS IN

Taking a few moments to think about the space you're having a conversation in and tailoring it for listening can be a powerful way to show someone that you're ready to pay attention to them. Before the start of a meeting, take a few minutes to make sure the chairs are laid out properly and that everyone has everything they need to be able to focus. Meeting to discuss a report? Be the one who says, 'I'll have a printed copy of the report in the room for you.' It can be as simple as putting some flowers on the table or arranging for coffee and biscuits, but the small touches that make the other person think that you have authentically thought about their needs can be powerful permissions for them to take the conversation more seriously and delve deeper in their thinking when it's then time for you to listen.

GETTING THE MOST FROM THE CONVERSATION

Active listening

The psychologist Carl Rogers coined the phrase 'active listening'. The idea of active listening, where you're working harder as a listener than you would be as a talker, is an inspiring idea. Active listening should convey that you are interested in that person and that their feelings are important to you. This is, of course, harder if you disagree, but the point is to honour the idea that the person you are listening to deserves to be understood.

Rogers describes listening as a kind act that, in itself, sends a message to the other person: 'While it is most difficult to convince someone that you respect him by telling him so, you are much more likely to get this message across by really behaving that way – by actually having and demonstrating respect for this person. Listening does this most effectively.'[2]

Listening is not the same as 'waiting to speak'. In many ways, active listening is the exact opposite. While we are just 'waiting to speak', we are in our own heads. We are focused on *our* narratives. Our agenda may be to steer the conversation away from the topic that the person we are listening to wants to talk about.

Watch out for phrases like:

- 'That happened to me too' (where you then start competing for who has the better story).
- 'Deepa! I haven't seen Deepa in aaaaaages… How is she?' (Which shifts the conversation away from the story and into a new conversation about the person mentioned.)
- 'That reminds me of a time…' (Effectively, you're saying your experiences are more interesting than the person who's talking.)
- (And worst of all): 'Sorry, just need to check my phone.'

Good listening is active. You could try offering a summary of what the other person has said, or regularly remind them with words or with body language that you are engaged and interested in what they have to say. Don't change the subject, offer opinions or shy away from your own discomfort. Good listening acknowledges the feelings behind the words and throws in questions only to further understand. Good listening resists the temptation to offer solutions. It's a natural temptation to want to offer a counter-argument or fix the problem. While there may be a time and a place for that, it comes later. It's not for while you're trying to understand what's being said.

Acknowledging the emotion

One of Rogers' ideas is that, in every conversation, there are two elements you're listening for – the information and the emotion. If an employee said to you, 'I've finished the report', you might reply with 'Great! Thank you!'. Whereas if instead they said, 'Man, that report is *finally* done', then your response of 'Great! Thank you!' would fall wide of the mark because that word '*finally*' tells you there's an emotion involved too – perhaps it's relief, or contempt, or stress, or something else. In active listening, you are trying to ensure you punctuate your listening with acknowledgements not just of the information, but of the emotion, too. Acknowledging the emotion tells the speaker that you connect with what they're feeling, that you understand them.

Roll with the pauses

If you want to be good at listening to other people, then you have to first be good at listening to yourself. And it's hard to do both at the same time. Great listening involves being comfortable with pauses – because you need space to listen to your own gathering thoughts after the other person has finished what they are telling you. Getting comfortable with pauses and silence takes practice, something Christopher Spence taught me all those years ago in my meetings with him.

One of the problems we face in conversations, particularly in our professional lives, is that they always seem to take place against a backdrop of speed. There's an unacknowledged but nagging truth in the room, that one or both parties need the conversation to be as short as possible because there's so much else to do. Yet we also know that depth and patience are critical for increasing our understanding. Slowing down and pausing allows us to listen more deeply. It also allows for more appreciation, memorizing, connection and – ultimately – more understanding.

Equal partnership

Everyone has the ability to think. It's important to approach every conversation with the starting point that, regardless of status, the two of you are equal thinking partners in it. Often what gets in the way of people's best thinking is a lack of ease or sense of psychological safety. This is particularly the case when there is an obvious power dynamic at play (such as meeting with the CEO of your company, whom you see only occasionally), or where there could be a subtle imbalance or bias due to status, race, gender, sexuality, class, age or culture. If you think you might be in a position of power or dominance over the other person, it's important to be mindful of this and make time at the beginning to put the other person at ease.

This is not to be under-estimated. It can be easy to forget how it felt much earlier in your career, when you walked into the offices of those with higher pay packets and more intimidating job titles. As you continue through your career, the chances are those memories fade, you get more comfortable in dealing with those situations and now, suddenly, *you're* the one in a senior position. The longer your career continues, the more of a blind spot you may have here.

Exercise: Curiosity in Listening

During a conversation, we often get swept along in the patterns of our own thinking. So, over the next few days, try to have some of these questions in your head before an in-depth conversation and see if you can pause and refer to them in your mind as you go back and forth in conversation. Remember to try and get to your own thinking after the other person has finished talking.

- What if I'm wrong?/What if we're wrong?
- What's most important?
- What's missing?
- How could we view this in a different way?
- What are the emotions that are underlying the content?
- How would other people I know be thinking about this same issue?
- Is this a pattern?
- How does what we are saying, or doing, sit with our values?
- What else might be going on here that I'm not hearing or might not be aware of?

Questions can also be great when they jump from being just in our own heads to being in the air. In those moments, asked directly of our partner, questions become helpers in clarifying our understanding of what's being said. A good question can even act as the guide or spark to sharpen or progress their thinking.

Avoid interruptions

Except for a few specific and well-purposed reasons, such as questioning to clarify, a good rule of thumb is to try not to interrupt. There are a number of negative effects of interruptions. The first is that it sends the signal to your partner that you're not fully allowing them the space to explain their thoughts or express their feelings. It can feel as if you are bored, impatient or not respecting what they have to say. Regular interruption can be frustrating and lead to someone closing down.

Second, lots of interruptions derail the conversation away from the final destination. When someone is regularly interrupted, it can feel like the destination they're trying to reach is less important than some minor distraction that the listener has fixated on – and now is asking them to make a detour to in the conversation.

And third, interruption can break the flow of thought and lead to a more shallow conversation. Sometimes the best parts of a conversation are those that are more difficult to find in the first few seconds. Like good coffee, you have to leave conversations to percolate and brew into something with depth.

Reflecting

Aside from interrupting to ask clarifying questions, the other exception to the rule of 'never interrupt' is when you are reflecting. Repeating back to someone what they've just told you shows them what they're thinking and feeling – and it can often be the first time they've heard their thoughts and feelings repeated out loud from someone else. You can do this in summary, by repeating or clarifying some of the key words or phrases, or offering some phrases of validation, like 'that must have been tricky', or 'I can't imagine what that must have felt like'.

For the person on the other end, it can feel like you're holding up a mirror and can help them to clarify their thoughts. My coach for many years, Rasheed Ogunlaru, would often use this technique to help me summarize my thoughts and connect it all together as a 'bigger picture'. And a choice word or phrase that summarizes things can help to create short-cuts and shorthand for future discussion on the same topic.

Language isn't just words

Our body language tells our conversation partner much more than we realize about what we really think: are we folding our arms, faced forward, or angling our shoulders to get ourselves out of the situation as quickly as possible? But there are many other non-verbal cues that we leave as well. Look out for gestures such as touching your face or fiddling with your hair, or focusing on the drink in front of you. Checking phones or shuffling paperwork are clear signs to your partner that you're not fully open. And of course, your partner may display all of these signs too. It's important to recognize when the level of discomfort is such that you need to suggest taking a break, or reset in some way. You can't listen deeply if your partner isn't ready to talk deeply.

Are you in 'story protection mode'?

If we have a particular interest in promoting a certain agenda, we can bias our listening towards this. For example, if you have worries about the environmental sustainability of the company you work for, you will listen for any messages from your CEO or senior leaders that support environmental considerations and perhaps ignore times when these considerations are not brought to the fore.

In one-to-one conversations, what this often looks like is accentuating the things that you agree on and skirting around those that might lead to disagreement or discomfort, with the aim of protecting the stories that you hold dear. You might also be aware of the stories that your partner is trying to protect too and skew the conversation to protect their stories. Of course, some of the stories that we protect are simply not true and when the truth does arrive, it feels more painful, so being aware of our own stories is ultimately an act of self-kindness as well as self-awareness.

Listening for what's missing

The management theorist Peter Drucker noted that 'the most important thing in communication is to hear what isn't being said'.[3] There are many reasons why someone might withhold the full story from you. They might feel nervous about your reaction or be unwilling to share their concerns about the performance of a colleague for fear of putting their colleague in a bad spot. Or they could be struggling with things in their personal life that they're determined to leave at the office door. Whatever the reason, it's important to stay curious to the idea that the most important thing you could learn today is not what you've already heard. There are three things to remember here that can help you cast the net wider and listen more deeply:

- Acknowledge the emotions you hear as well as the facts (particularly if those emotions feel disconnected from the content, or feel like a 'leakage', as we talked about earlier).
- Leave plenty of space. Don't be in a hurry to jump back in and respond. Often the best parts of my podcast interviews are when I give someone the space to talk. The big truths usually follow lots of smaller ones.
- Ask questions, using a mix of open and incisive styles. Open questions ('what's happening?') are great for creating the space for your partner to explore their thoughts and as they do, you might stumble across something important, or at least the hint of something that might be more significant than it's given the words to be. Direct and incisive questions ('so, would you be interested in that new role?') are great to hone in on what you might be hearing, either to confirm or deny.

Managing Difficult Conversations with Kindness

The hardest conversations are often the ones that will deepen a relationship, or bring about the most profound shifts, and yet despite knowing this logically, they're also often the ones that we shy away from. It's fair to say most people find it deeply uncomfortable talking and listening when there are strong feelings at play and our lizard brains fear things like conflict, a sense of powerlessness, disagreements or disconnected expectations. The good news is that you don't have to avoid these kinds of conversations – and the more you practice, the easier they get. What follows are a few tools and mindset shifts that can help when it gets heavy.

BEING A CONTAINER

When someone is in a highly emotional state, the quality of your listening skills is much like holding a crying baby. Here, your aim is to provide a container for the emotions, to let them be expressed in a way that hopefully moves quickly from extreme discomfort to one of comfort and feeling soothed. If you're someone with natural empathy, it's likely that what you are being told will affect your own emotional state as you listen. In doing so, be aware that your job is to be a strong container. Your partner needs help, in this moment, to get back from the 'Lizard Brain' and eventually return to the 'Logic Brain'. If your reaction is to meet what they're telling you with your own very emotional response, you can cease to be a container for their emotions and leave them feeling overwhelmed as they now feel they need to help you manage your emotions too. It's a difficult balance to strike: it's important to show empathy, to reflect the emotions and to care, but it's also important to maintain your focus on keeping the space safe enough for them to express what they want to say.

TAKING BLAME OFF THE TABLE

Our human tendency to tell stories often leads to the temptation to attach blame to a specific person or event. Stories require simplicity and the honing of complexity down to simpler forms but in reality, most things that go wrong do so for a number of different reasons.

In psychotherapy, there is a model called the 'systemic' field. Taking a systemic view can be a very useful way to approach difficult conversations because it helps us add explanations to decisions or actions that initially seemed to have none. It reminds us to take a broader view, and one that is less personal.

At its heart, its hypothesis is that most things that end up becoming problems started out as the attempted solution to something else. We might have caused a safety breach because of a need somewhere else to cut financial corners. We may have replaced beloved ways of serving our clients because of a drive towards more streamlined or digital solutions. Decisions – and indeed our feelings – take place as part of complex systems and it's much more likely something in the system has driven us towards the problem that we are now facing. We can also look to change or address the flaws that are in the system, but only by understanding them more fully first. That's why listening deeply is so important.

Listening deeply is the definition of a kind act

When we are in a conversation, the quality of our attention determines the quality of our listening and in turn, this influences the quality of the other person's thinking. Listening is far from a passive activity; being a good listener is in itself a kind act. But just as with kindness, being a good listener is a verb, not a noun. It's not something that any of us arrive at by accident; it's by applying deliberate principles, techniques and mindsets to help get the best out of every conversation. It takes a level of vulnerability to listen well, because as we enter the space to listen, we should do so with the idea in our minds that we're willing to be changed.

KINDFUL HERO: CASE STUDY
RACHEL FORDE, CEO OF UM LONDON: 'IF PEOPLE
ARE LISTENED TO, THEY FEEL VALUED.'

Rachel Forde is the CEO of creative media agency UM London and has spent the last 20 years or so driving client growth, while also focusing on culture in some of the world's biggest media agencies. Under her leadership, UM has seen impressive annual revenue growth of 30 per cent, while at the same time she has halved the company's gender pay gap and transitioned her board from being 85 per cent male to achieving a 50:50 male/female split.

Rachel says the most important trait she has as a leader is her empathy: 'When you look at some of the leaders recently who have been successful or not, then it really is all about kindness. In the past, kindness was very much seen as a soft skill, but these days, people understand that it builds empathy, trust and loyalty. But the problem is when you've got an overflowing inbox and back-to-back meetings every day, you have to prioritize the time to take time out to listen. And you have to make it part of the DNA of the culture too.'

At UM, Rachel has set up something called the Leadership Council. One layer down from the board, it started out as an open-agenda forum to listen to staff, to get everyone into the habits both of talking and listening. The Leadership Council has been the catalyst for several off-shoot groups that have aimed to help everyone build community, talk, listen and understand each other's unique perspectives. UM now has internal groups, such as the:

- Ability Squad
- Heritage Squad
- Parenting Squad
- LGBTQ Squad.

Rachel says: 'We have lots of different communities – listening communities. It can't be a tick-box thing, it has to start with "How do you want to talk about this?" and asking people "How do you want to engage?". Those "squads" are all about recognizing diversity, and the importance of belonging, with the aim that everyone feels valued and sees the organization as a place they can be heard and understood.'

But Rachel also uses listening as a way to drive some pretty impressive growth, too: 'We have really practical ones like Speed Squad, which looks at questions like "How can we speed things up?", "How can we get rid of stuff that isn't important?", "What would give you more time in your day?", "What's blocking you?" and so on. Our mantra with everything is "What can we do better?" and the only way to figure that out is by listening.'

At the end of the Covid pandemic, Rachel set up a company-wide initiative called MyCoach. This gave every employee, regardless of their place in the company, an opportunity to participate in three hours of coaching. She also briefly closed the entire business down so that everyone was forced to take five days out to rest and recuperate: 'It was about saying to them, "Look, it's been a really stressful time. Have some time out and rest." And then with the coaching, we were saying, "These hours are for you, to talk about work, home, whatever it is." And we knew that some of those people might go into those three hours of coaching and be deciding, "Actually, we don't wanna work in media anymore", but it's about being brave enough to know that what you ultimately want is a happy and engaged workforce. It has to be focused on the people. If you use this people-first lens, then the results just follow. And it also makes you more informed and impactful in all the decisions that you make.'

Questions for Reflection

* Who in your life makes you feel heard and valued?
* Do your colleagues have space to talk (and you space to listen to them) without agenda? If so, is it regular enough? If not, how could you create these spaces?
* What do you think it feels like to be on the other side of you? Do you think people feel heard? What can you improve?

Kindness Challenge: Listening Partnerships

This week's challenge is all about rethinking how we listen. Recruit one person (a friend or colleague) and choose one subject (it can be the thing that just happened that you need to get your head around, or something future-focused and strategic). Go for a walk together. At the start of the walk, say your hellos and catch up with each other then one of you should become the talker and the other person becomes the listener. Take on these roles for five to ten minutes, then swap around.

* As the talker: Talk in a relaxed and free-flowing way about that subject. Stay on topic. Include your feelings about it, not just the facts. Pause in silence whenever you need to.
* As the listener: Listen. Don't add anything, except 'uh-huhs', or body language that shows that you're paying attention. Hold the space for your partner to talk comfortably.

At the end, discuss what you both learned from both roles.

'THE KEY TO ANY SUCCESSFUL BUSINESS IS TO GIVE PEOPLE THE FREEDOM TO FEEL UNIQUE, BUT AT THE SAME TIME, THE SENSE OF BELONGING TO FEEL PART OF SOMETHING BIGGER.'

JANET LEIGHTON, DIRECTOR OF HAPPINESS, TIMPSON

Graham Allcott

4. People First, Work Second. Always.

PEOPLE

WORK

#1

It's much easier to perform to a high level in our jobs when we have stability in our lives: good health, a stable and comfortable home and the support of our friends, families and key relationships are all vital components of our success. Our organizations benefit from the stability of our personal lives, because it means we have more headspace, time and energy to commit to the cause. But what about when this isn't the case? What if a colleague is going through something difficult, like an illness, divorce or bereavement? This is one of the most pressing opportunities for kindness.

People aren't machines and when someone is having one of those tricky patches in life, it's not a realistic expectation that they should still maintain peak work performance. We can choose not to see these moments as a massive inconvenience to the work (even though someone's absence might, of course, cause disruption), but instead to see them as a golden opportunity to show that person how valued, supported and cared for they are.

Here is the first of three chapters focusing on our approach to people. 'People First, Work Second. Always' has been a personal mantra of mine for many years. It has become the de-facto approach that we take at Think

Productive to dealing with people's difficult personal stuff, as well as being adopted by some of our clients, too. It has also come to stand for something much wider than just personal-crisis-management – it's about the importance of dignity, work–life balance and a mutual sense of commitment in any employee relationship or business partnership.

The Origins of 'People First, Work Second. Always.'

In the early 2000s, Jamie Oliver created his social enterprise restaurant, Fifteen. The idea was to bring together young people from difficult backgrounds with very little work experience and invest heavily in them so that they were able to take on jobs as chefs and waiting staff. The process was recorded for a Channel 4 documentary, *Jamie's Kitchen*, and there was one scene that had a profound impact on my approach to managing people. One of Oliver's trainees arrived for work in tears, having had a row with her partner. It was clear that she was in a vulnerable emotional state, inconducive to the cut and thrust of life in a busy kitchen. Oliver spent some time with her, gave her a hug and sent her home. He was clear that what she needed in that moment wasn't to soldier on, but to take a step back. Oliver had a kitchen to run and knew he'd be a person short, but his instinct was that a pressured day in a hot kitchen probably wasn't the best thing for her mental health – and might actually have caused more problems in the kitchen too.

'People First, Work Second. Always' started life as my way of bringing that kind and compassionate approach to dealing with people's crisis moments. The idea is simple: no matter how busy you are, no matter how many demands your customers place on you, it creates a golden rule that people always come first when you get 'the call'.

I'm sure you know what I mean by 'the call': over the years I've had many of these calls. Some are actual calls, some are sat face to face in a meeting room or café, others are text messages or WhatsApp voice notes. They all contain a version of being told, 'Houston, we have a problem'. It might be the death of a close relative, a serious accident, the diagnosis of a scary illness, or being stranded after a cancelled plane.

When 'the call' comes, the starting point should always be the person first. The needs of the organization take a back seat, no matter the consequences. It's easy to forget that the person making 'the call' will likely be nervous about the conversation, too. They don't want to rock the boat, or cause disruption. If they're ill, then like you, they wish they weren't. An important part of our response is to calm their Lizard Brains and allay their fear and guilt. Their negative self-talk has probably been in overdrive thinking about 'the call' and our job is to prove that self-talk wrong.

I remember when a colleague told me she was pregnant. Weeks beforehand we had agreed a new role for her – a significant promotion, with lots of responsibility. She was just getting into her stride in the new role when she got the news. We of course arranged her maternity leave and cover for her role so that she could transition back after her leave. Not once had it crossed my mind that this affected her new role. Much later, I found out that despite our many conversations about 'People First, Work Second. Always' being our approach, her own self-talk was worried that it wouldn't apply to her, or at least not this time. From that, I learned to always assume a level of nervousness and personal jeopardy, whatever your policies or reputation – these are big life moments.

If someone has been a loyal employee and has been committed to the cause for a period of time, then 'People First, Work Second. Always' is about saying to that person, 'You've been committed to us, now let us show you what that means the other way.' It means you start with what that person needs. If that is sometimes longer than what your company's policy says, then you go to HR or find another way to do it (or *don't* go to HR and just find a way to do it!). I've had several instances, as a business owner, where taking care of people comes directly out of my own pocket. But even then, it's a price worth paying because when you get 'the call', it's usually a giant version of 'the gap'. It's one of the biggest opportunities for kindness, where the stakes are high and in a moment in that person's life when they need you the most. If you can show kindness when the pressure is high, this will be remembered.

'Always' Means No Exceptions

The 'Always' is the most important word in this mantra. It means no exceptions. No matter how busy, no matter how much you think you need that person on that day, when you both take a step back, they get what they really need and you'll always figure it out later in the background. Your team will rally. It seems impossible or stressful at the time and usually when you receive that news that someone has a problem and needs to step out, you're in the middle of a work day, looking at ten other things that feel like they're not where you need them to be. But what I've learned over the years is that ultimately, you do figure it out.

'Always' Means Sacrifice

In a 'People First, Work Second. Always' moment, there are often simple phrases that carry a lot of meaning. For example, a phrase like 'take as long as you need' comes from a place of love. You're giving them the gift of space. Of time and care. You're also placing trust in them, declaring that you believe in their level of commitment to the work, to the relationship they have with you and to the rest of the team.

It's a loaded phrase on the other end, too. It's you saying, 'I'm prepared to find a way around this and to cope with you being out of action for as long as you need that to be.' Often it has financial implications. As you say those words, it often commits you to many hours of sacrifice – the projects you won't get to work on, the extra hours you might have to put in – all of which are very real costs to this approach.

Saying 'Just tell us when you're ready' or 'we trust you' places autonomy but also responsibility on the person taking time away from work. It's a ceding of control and power, so that you can put them first.

It's Always Somebody's 'Always'

The word 'always' is also a reminder that it's always *somebody's* 'always'. There's always someone on your team who needs some support. I remember a time when it felt like we were using the 'People First, Work Second. Always' mantra a lot at Think Productive. For a while we started saying that we thought our company was cursed, such were the frequency of traumatic life events that seemed to beset our small team – everyone had parenting issues, health problems, operations, deaths in the family, accidents, stressful breakups, ceilings caving in… you name it. We were predominantly young, fit and active people, but still these catastrophes kept appearing, one after the other. All we wanted was a stretch of 'normal' where everyone was happy and safe at the same time. But then you realize that in life suffering *is* normal; shittiness and bad luck are part of the deal. It's not that circumstances aren't always ideal, it's that they *rarely are*.

Remembering that it's 'always somebody's always' is useful. When planning workloads, we tend to assume that we will always have everyone working at their full capacity, but the real world isn't like this. It's also useful because it helps us to have a radar for the things that people might be enduring quietly. It reminds us to try and spot 'the gaps' and be supportive before someone reaches crisis point. Recognizing that 'It's always somebody's always' is hard. Especially in the frenetic pace of day-to-day working life.

Phil is a senior engineer and he told me about a time when he was under a lot of stress, working on a huge electric car project for Jaguar Land Rover. Every week he had to report to his bosses about the work of his team. The stakes could not have been higher – the future of the company would of course be electric and this was the big statement to the market. His direct report had sent him an update that he knew his bosses would be unhappy with. It also felt like progress had slowed and things just weren't right. Phil did what we've all done in stressful situations before – he started bashing out an angry email. And then before he could send it, he was interrupted. By the time he returned to his desk to read his draft, it read less like the perfect resonance of his anger and more like a shitty email he'd get from someone else. He deleted the draft and instead sent back a simple one-liner: 'Are you OK?' That short email opened up a conversation about stress. The person did indeed need support. He started to reorganize and redistribute the work. Things began to move more quickly again: 'I know that if I had sent that original email, I'd have caused a lot of damage to that relationship. Probably permanent damage, perhaps even fatal to that working relationship,' he told me.

As we plan the work of the team, it's our job to leave enough space and flexibility. It's fair to assume that there's almost always someone who needs time away. When it's someone's turn because something in their life needs their attention, it's up to everyone else to step up and cover for them. That's the deal. And then when it's *your* always, the idea is 'what goes around, comes around'. That's part of the deal, too. You get to step away without guilt, knowing the expectation is that others will cover for you while you fix your broken roof, or your broken heart, or your family crisis. Knowing that everyone has your back at work allows you to place your attention where it's most needed in that moment. It empowers you to give it your fullest attention – it means you're not the person nipping out from the funeral to send emails.

'Why Not Soldier On? Surely the World Needs Us?'

What we're often taught when it comes to illnesses, mental health and other personal issues is that the 'professional' thing to do is to 'soldier on'. The British culture of a 'stiff upper lip', or the spirit of 'keep calm and carry on' are particularly pervasive – that may have been a great propaganda tool to avoid people dwelling on mental health in a war, but let's remember business is not a war and we are not required to 'soldier on'.

At the heart of this truth is something very sad for us, though. It's a good thing for our egos to feel useful, needed or even indispensable. We see this as a reflection of our value to the organization and of course in turn as a reflection of our own self-worth. When Elon Musk was asked by the *Wall Street Journal* why he has remained CEO of Tesla for so long, despite his pronouncements that he is 'not interested in being boss of anything', he said, 'I have to, frankly, or Tesla is going to die.'[1] While emotionally, this kind of superhero narrative feels compelling to all involved (for Musk, it offers purpose and meaning; for those around him, it offers the ability to believe that there's a magical 'adult in the room' who has all the answers), it could be seen a different way – it's bad management. It shows a lack of succession planning and a careless attitude to managing risk, if a company would literally 'die' without one person in it.

There's a mini-version of this Muskian fantasy playing out in all of our heads. We want to feel indispensable. Within my own business, I've worked hard to create the structures that mean I have the freedom to step away (I took a full year's sabbatical a few years ago and didn't look at my work emails once. The business grew!), but at the same time, finding out that you're not quite as unique and indispensable as you thought is tinged with sadness, too. We derive meaning and purpose from our work. And because we do, it's easy to see why we over-inflate its importance and in turn our individual importance to the work.

So 'People First, Work Second. Always' starts from an assumption that the person *does* care about the job they do – and probably too much! People want to feel needed and that's why when they're forced to step away, it can create genuine pain and even mourning.

> **'I ASSOCIATE "KIND" WITH GOOD LEADERSHIP. THINKING BACK TO PEOPLE I'VE WORKED WITH IN ACADEMIA, THE ONES WHO ARE VERY SUCCESSFUL TEND TO BE THE PEOPLE WHO ARE GENUINELY EMPATHETIC AND KIND.'**
>
> **Dr Cal Newport, author of Deep Work**

The Magic of Dignity

'People First, Work Second. Always' is really just another way of saying, 'I choose dignity'. Yes, we are all unique and have our own weirdnesses – different skills, interests, qualities and flaws – but also, we all need to feel respected, valued, loved and believed in. We long to feel trusted and invested in. We want to take pride in looking after ourselves as well as in contributing to something bigger. And we want to feel a sense of community and connection with the people around us, too. Moments of connection can be surprisingly small and yet still create huge impact for people.

Colin Bennett is a national development manager at the English Football League (EFL) Trust: 'I had a ropey end to the year and just when I didn't need it, we had a full organization virtual meeting. I wasn't looking forward to it and reluctantly joined. A couple of colleagues from different teams both said, "Brilliant, Colin is here, I am so pleased to see you" (or words to that effect). My mood lifted instantly and I felt welcomed, wanted and needed. I contacted them later after the meeting and said how much that meant as they didn't know what I was going through and both were gobsmacked because they were just behaving as they would like people to behave with them. There was no hidden agenda, just them displaying kindness as part of who they are.'

Human Beings versus Humans Doing

When I started Think Productive, I made a conscious effort to build a community around the work, with a strong spirit of collaboration. I started hearing phrases like 'The TP Family' or people saying, 'Nah, we're doing it the TP way' or 'That decision wasn't very TP'. It struck me that defining what 'the TP way' even meant in those circumstances was no longer something that only I had ownership of: it was a collective sense. But what it has come to mean over the years is a multitude of the qualities that we seek to model and encourage: listening, honesty, clarity, transparency, empathy, consultation and yes, doing the kind thing as well as the right thing.

We try our best to listen: we do 1-2-1s either every month or every couple of weeks (whatever feels like the most appropriate cadence) with everybody; we celebrate birthdays but also milestones, like when one of our team members – Lee – finally got the house move he needed after two years of things falling through or being difficult. We give people space to air concerns or issues; we actively try to dismantle processes or cancel or renegotiate work that feels like it adds more stress than value; we ask people to talk about how they're feeling and what else is going on for them.

Kindfulness at Work is about building a community that feels diverse and where difference is celebrated, yet at the same time also feels as if like-minded humans are coming together to do something bigger than the sum of our parts and with a set of shared values. Why build a team when you can build a community instead?

Exercise: Humans Being

The next time you have a team gathering (preferably in the same room, but online is fine), spend some time 'just being' with each other. Take away the pressure for there to be an agenda or any work to do and get to know each other a bit more personally. If you're the person in charge of the meeting, make sure that you allocate equal talking time to everyone. It's helpful to have a structure for this or a question to discuss (otherwise it can just feel a bit awkward), so here are a few ideas to get you started:

- 'If you could be anywhere else in the world right now instead of here, where would you be?'
- On a piece of paper, draw your personal coat of arms. Ask every-one to draw a shield and then in each quarter of the shield, they draw something that means a lot to them – it could be a person, a hobby, a place, a value, or whatever else they choose.
- 'What are you most proud of?'
- 'Hope and fears for the year ahead?'
- (And with teams where everyone knows each other quite well): Go around the table and ask each person to say one thing they admire or value about the person to their left.

What I'm hoping you will find is that small moments of connection and kindness can super-charge the positive motivation of a team very quickly and create a sense of trust and connection.

KINDNESS HERO: CASE STUDY
EMILY CHANG, CEO OF THE MCCANN WORLD GROUP

Emily Chang is the CEO of the McCann World Group, a 400+ person marketing agency based in Shanghai. She's previously held senior roles at Apple, Starbucks and the Intercontinental Hotel Group. Emily leads with incredible grace and kindness and is the embodiment of the 'People First, Work Second. Always' mantra.

Emily uses her personal life as a signifier to employees about the kind of person they're allowed to be at work. Her book, *The Spare Room*,[2] tells the story of Emily opening up the spare room of her house to a young homeless girl she saw at the side of the road – and realizing that this was something that she could continue to do, over and over again. She has now looked after 17 young people via her spare room, but also sees 'the spare room' as a euphemism for the question 'what can you offer?'.

A leader who tells stories, she is full of humanity, inspiring loyalty and peak performance from those around her. She told me how when one of her direct reports had relocated from the US to work with her in Shanghai, leaving behind his wife and two children, it was clear that he was missing home and didn't have the budget or spare annual leave to make a trip back. Without him knowing, Emily managed to find some budget so that he could visit them and also so that in future they could come out to visit him as well. But Emily went the extra mile, too. She got her children involved to help her create a 'Welcome Home' banner, to break the news in style. I asked Emily what had prompted her own behaviour around kindness and she quickly told me the story of her boss, Kenneth McPherson, CEO of InterContinental Hotel Group in EMEA: 'I'd been trying so hard to adopt this little boy and it had taken all of my energy outside of work. I remember one day Kenneth asking to see me in his office and when I arrived, he was there with the head of HR and he seemed nervous. I had no idea what the meeting was about so I was suddenly pretty nervous too!

'He passes this paper across the table to me. And he said, "I'd like you to read that." I opened the paper and it says, "IHG Group would like to help you with adoption fees". And I'm reading it and my eyes are welling up. I looked at him and he said to me, "I was so touched by what you're doing with this boy, I asked HR and I realized we don't have a policy to help people, especially international employees adopt local Chinese children, so we'd like to give you this small token that will help you with the adoption fees."

'That allowed me to have some time off to let my new arrival settle into the home and made me feel like what I was doing was on a par with any mother giving birth the conventional way. That single act of kindness stayed with me because it was so personal and so beyond the call of duty for a CEO. This is the thing that builds deep loyalty and affinity. And loyalty is not a word to be used lightly in this day and age, but if Kenneth McPherson called me, I would drop everything and do whatever he needed, because he touched me in such an incredibly deep way.'

Emily's natural warmth and love of people is infectious, even just being on a Zoom call with her. And it's clear that her example is followed by others in her team. She told me: 'I looked over my admin's shoulder the other day and she had all these pictures of turkeys on her desk. Thanksgiving isn't a massively celebrated holiday in China, so I said, "Hey, what's with the turkeys?" She said, "Oh, we have our monthly Happy Hour coming up and I was thinking it'd be a great opportunity to print out little cardboard turkeys and have everybody write something they're thankful for, for somebody else." I loved the idea and I love that she just comes up with it and knows that she has free rein to do this without even having to ask.'

Emily pays forward the kindness shown to her and creates the culture where she creates the ripples for others, too: 'I have this thing where whenever I stay in hotels, I use the hotel stationery to write a handwritten note to someone. Recently, people have started to pass it on. I had a quick touch base with a colleague about somebody in our team who's making a career move. And my colleague said, "Well, I really wish her luck. I think this is the right move for her, it's the right move for our business." And then she looked at me with a little smile and said, "Guess what I did? I wrote her a handwritten note! I have the note you wrote me from your hotel pinned at my desk so I wrote her a note, just to say thank you for resigning in such a respectful way. I think this is a great move for you and I wish you the best." And that young girl will probably carry that with her. So yeah, I think kindness does amplify, there's a ripple effect. And what's amazing is a lot of times, we may not see those ripples two or three people along the chain, but we know that they're there.'

Other ways to build dignity & foster the 'People First, Work Second. Always.' ethos

Of course, the first way to ensure a 'people first' approach is to take it at the face value we discussed at the start of this piece: use the 'always' to mean no exceptions and as a reminder that it's always somebody's always. But there are some other things you can do that give people more dignity and sense of belonging in their workplace.

1 Celebrate birthdays and milestones

In many ways, the easiest place to start is to remember – and celebrate – birthdays. At the same time, it's good to remember that not everyone likes cake, or beer, or even a card. As you'll discover later in Principle Six, it's important to 'treat people the way THEY want to be treated', so putting a tiny bit of thought into this can make a big difference, too. And when people get their first house, or first dog, or have just overcome a period of struggle, then let them know they're seen and heard.

2 Get beyond compassionate leave policies

Most large organizations have broken policies for compassionate leave that are just detached from the reality of family life. They give people small numbers of days off but only if certain specific types of relative are ill or pass away. These policies often say nothing about non-traditional family structures and don't serve people for whom their closest relative is a grandparent or non-blood relative. Good managers start with genuine compassion and work from there, often bypassing entirely what's in the policy.

3 Explaining their greatness

One of the best ways for people to feel a sense of dignity and connection in their work is to explain it to others. Asking people to explain their work (especially up the hierarchy, such as presenting to the board or senior management) is a great opportunity to build confidence and recognize the unique contribution each person makes. It's also, for many people, a unique opportunity to take a step back from the day-to-day busy-ness and ask questions like 'how does my work fit in?', 'what are we achieving?', or 'how is this useful?'.

4 Go with their flow, not yours

When it comes to managing people, it's often assumed that a manager needs to have all the answers, but sometimes the best way to lead is by asking good questions. Sharing the decision-making and giving people more control over how, where and when they do their work are all ways of showing more trust in your colleagues. Sometimes the kindest – and most productive – thing is to get out of the way and let people get on with being brilliant.

5 Create the regular windows to reduce the awkwardness

One of the items on our directors' meeting agenda at Think Productive is 'personal download'. We use this to make sure there's a regular moment for us to reconnect with each other's human experiences. In our staff 1-2-1s too, there's a whole section about 'what is going on in your life?'. It can be awkward to bring up personal struggles, but having a moment every month that reminds people that it's OK to talk about it means it's never lost. Over the years, they have told me some pretty life-changing bits of news in those moments and it's a great way to normalize the idea that we can show up at work without having to put up a robotic facade.

Do People Ever Abuse the Trust?

I've sometimes had pushback when sharing this mantra ('*Reeeally* always? For *everyone*?!'). Here, it's worth saying that the starting premise for this approach is a mutual sense of trust, where you're pretty confident in someone's general dedication and intention to be productive when they can be. It assumes a level of honesty and personal integrity too, but that's all part of living with an abundance mentality instead of one of scarcity and assuming the best in people as a default rather than the worst.

Are there times, with extremely dissatisfied employees, or where trust has been repeatedly broken, where you may need to operate a different way? Sure. But I can honestly say there's only been one incident, across everyone I've ever worked with, where I felt someone had abused this way of working – where they were prepared to take as much time and space as was offered (and then some!) but never prepared to reciprocate and pitch in to help others on the other side of it.

In that situation, that person was also under-performing anyway and wasn't particularly engaged in their work. Keeping the culture consistent for everyone meant a cost of a few days in sick pay for that person that they shouldn't have been paid, but beyond that, it was just a case of an employee who wasn't a great fit for the organization and after a couple of amicable conversations, they moved on to a new career. I'll happily take the hit of occasional over-leniency if that's the price we pay for a kind culture that puts people first. The benefits for everybody else, in terms of team morale, engagement and performance, are clear and far outweigh the occasional bit of extra sick pay.

Ultimately, it comes back to the notion of operating from a place of abundance rather than scarcity: if you want people to trust you, start by trusting them. If you want to create a culture where people feel valued, start by valuing them as people. And if you want people to take their work seriously, take their lives seriously in return.

Kindfulness recognizes the importance of humanity at work. When you put people first and their dignity at the centre of everything, it builds the trust and psychological safety that drives performance.

Questions for Reflection

- What happens in your organization/team when someone is in crisis?
- How can you help people feel safe enough and valued enough to be themselves at work?
- Which agendas, narratives or people might get in the way, or not support the idea of 'People First, Work Second. Always.'?

Kindness Challenge: Dignity as Kindness

This week, I want you to focus on acts of kindness that honour the unique humanity of your team. Nothing to do with helping them with their work and everything to do with seeing them as people. Pay special attention to where you might be able to spot 'the gap' in places you might have missed it just a few weeks ago. As you're practising kindness, you're likely to notice more than ever before. Here are a few ideas:

1 If someone is showing a lot of signs of being preoccupied (taking phone calls, staring into space, scrolling, looking tired), then ask them what's wrong.

2 If you don't do this already, have a regular focus on people's lives, mental health and general welfare as a question during 1-2-1 supervision meetings or lunches.

3 Talk about 'People First, Work Second. Always.' with your team. What do they think about this approach? Use it as an excuse to talk to your team about trust, commitment and motivation. What comes up here that you need to work on?

4 Think about and implement some small but regular rituals where you can add dignity and individuality and help people celebrate positive life events such as birthdays, engagements and house moves. Create the space for the team to be a witness for each other's lives.

5 Apply it as readily to your own life as you do your team's. When do you need to take a break? Remember our first principle: Kindness starts with you.

'WE LEARNED ABOUT GRATITUDE AND HUMILITY – THAT SO MANY PEOPLE HAD A HAND IN OUR SUCCESS, FROM THE TEACHERS WHO INSPIRED US TO THE JANITORS WHO KEPT OUR SCHOOL CLEAN, AND WE WERE TAUGHT TO VALUE EVERYONE'S CONTRIBUTION AND TREAT EVERYONE WITH RESPECT.'

MICHELLE OBAMA

Graham Allcott

5. Be Humble

NK Chaudhary is the founder of Jaipur Rugs, one of India's leading exporters of hand-woven rugs. Founded in 1978, it's now a multi-million-dollar operation, with a network of 40,000 rug weavers and customers in 40 countries. There are many textiles companies in India, but Chaudhary's story and operating model are unique: kindness and humility are at the epicentre of all he has built. Chaudhary sees business as 'a form of self-actualization'. His ability to see business as a way of alleviating poverty – and turn the business model of his industry on its head – is one of the many characteristics that sets him apart and his humble nature and obvious social conscience are why he has often been dubbed 'The Gandhi of Business'. His philosophy can be encapsulated in his view that: 'Let goodness, fairness, and most importantly, love prevail in business – profits will inevitably follow.'

KINDNESS HERO: CASE STUDY
NK CHAUDHARY, FOUNDER OF JAIPUR RUGS (INDIA)

NK Chaudhary started Jaipur Rugs against the wishes of his parents. From a middle-class background, he'd turned down a steady job working in a bank to instead start his business with a small loan and nine weavers ready to help him produce his first rugs. Weaving was an occupation for the 'untouchables', the uneducated village people that the majority of the Indian caste system looks down upon. Most weavers were exploited by the middlemen and company owners who sold their products; the end result was a system in which sweatshop labour conditions didn't allow for career expression, let alone career progression. Weavers were predominantly female, badly treated and often forced to leave grandparents or neighbours to care for their children while they travelled miles from the family home to work long shifts in appalling conditions for low wages.

The Jaipur Rugs model has turned this on its head. In the early days of the business, Chaudhary began talking to his first weavers, seeking to understand their personal lives and their concerns and ambitions. He focused on how to create dignity, good working conditions and job satisfaction for his employees. This meant challenging the assumptions that the deeply-rooted caste system in India had created.

The idea that changed everything was deceptively simple: instead of requiring weavers to work full-time shifts miles away from home, what if they could work flexibly, closer to home or even at home? He abandoned the big factory model. In its place, he instituted a decentralized model, focusing on the needs of the weavers, not on his needs as the owner. He invested in more looms and began distributing them to the villages and homes that his employees lived in. By putting trust in his employees – to look after the looms, work flexibly, train others and bring creative ideas for new rug designs – many felt he was taking too big a risk, but it is this artisan-focused model that has been at the heart of the success of Jaipur Rugs to this day. Despite the size of the operation, Chaudhary still takes the time to listen to the rank-and-file weavers and hear their concerns and ideas: 'If my weavers are happy, they will do good work. Good work is good for business,' he told me. For Chaudhary, such humility has made him not only revered, but also very rich.

Genuine humility is a magnetic trait. Humble people also get results, in ways that might surprise you. A study from the *Journal of Positive Psychology*[1] found a correlation between humility and helpfulness – and we increase our motivation to perform in a job when we feel that our manager is there to help us.

Humility is often defined as the opposite of arrogance or narcissism, or as being relatively down-to-earth and capable of understanding one's own strengths and weaknesses appropriately. In a society and working culture that has traditionally rewarded those who exaggerate or assert dominance, it can be striking and extremely effective when someone cedes some of their own power or advantage in order to elevate others. US President Harry S. Truman perfectly summed up humility when he said, 'It is amazing what you can accomplish if you don't care who gets the credit.'[2]

Here, we are going to look at humility. We'll cover why it's a trait to be encouraged and developed and the art of being the spotlight, not the star. And since the best way to be more humble is to practice humility, we'll run through some scripts for you to try in your own role.

Humility Gets Results

Humility is something the prolific entrepreneur Michael Norton CBE has lived out for the past 30 years. Norton's early career was in merchant banking and publishing, but it's in the voluntary sector that his influence is most obvious. Large organizations like The Directory of Social Change, Changemakers, UnLtd and MyBank are among the dozens of organizations that he has founded in his career. The secret? To start things you want to make happen and support them, but then don't worry about who gets the credit. He told me about his work developing financial literacy in schools and its journey to become the award-winning charity, MyBank: 'I started it then and managed to find a bit of seed funding, but then I met Lily Lapenna. She's gone on to develop this idea into a thriving social enterprise, she's received an MBE and taken it to the next level. If you get out of the way, that's where the magic happens.'

Humility where you feel you should least expect it is particularly powerful. Paul Grubb, Regional Creative Director at the advertising agency GTB in South East Asia, told me about his time working with John Webster, one of the most famous TV commercial writers in the world: 'Sitting and having a social drink with him, he would tell me about something he'd just done and laugh to himself that he thought it was funny, but then say, "I'm not entirely sure, I'd really like your opinion; do you think it's any good?" When I was in my twenties, this to me was the equivalent of James Cameron asking me how I thought he should compose the next camera shot! His humility was inspiring.'

> ## 'KEEP YOUR HEAD UP IN FAILURE, AND YOUR HEAD DOWN IN SUCCESS.'
>
> **Jerry Seinfeld, stand-up comedian**

WHY HUMILITY IS GOOD

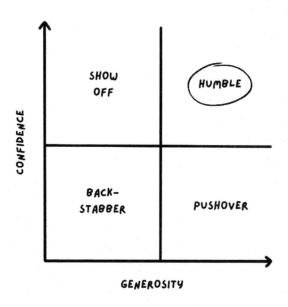

Let's think about humility as based on two features:

- Someone's confidence in their own skills
- Their sense of generosity.

Humility is Strength

To be truly humble starts from an awareness of your own power and strength. It's a conscious decision – to approach someone kindly in a way that doesn't try to dominate and deliberately puts their needs front and centre. The starting point is a combination of confidence and generosity. Humility operates from an abundance mentality and rejects the notion that the fastest way to success is by being a superstar, or a 'business baddie'.

PUSHOVERS, BACK-STABBERS AND SHOW-OFFS

When we are lacking in generosity, or don't have the confidence in our own skills, then of course we get something else. Without confidence, those who are highly generous become pushovers. They end up being taken advantage of, because they are unable to communicate in a way that recognizes their skills or contribution, or are unable to put in place the boundaries that stop their generosity being abused.

And without generosity, it's easy for confidence and self-protection to become overbearing and someone ends up becoming a show-off. Almost nobody in the world who receives kudos or material success does so completely of their own accord. While someone's personal skill or hard graft will be a factor, other factors like a brilliant team, luck, privilege, mentoring and many other things will also play a part. Being a show-off is ungenerous because it's ultimately about denying these parts of the story in favour of the personal glory – and it's also a refusal to pass on the 'leg-up' that they themselves have received. And with neither confidence in their own skills nor a sense of generosity, people are left to resort to the ultimate self-protection: back-stabbing. Cultures where people seek to undermine each other and where conflict is high quickly become distracted from the work and so much of the time of an organization is taken up sorting out the in-fighting, or trying to reach consensus.

So just like kindness itself, humility starts with you – from self-awareness and self-confidence: self-awareness, so that you have an idea how your actions affect those around you, and self-confidence so that you've appraised your skillset and you feel secure that you are bringing value to your team.

Healthy levels of humility lead to a high-performing team, whereas a lack of generosity or confidence can predicate a toxic culture without clear boundaries and where individuals' needs are prioritized over the needs of the team or the work. Humility is only possible when the foundations of confidence and generosity are in place.

'THE KINDER I AM ABLE TO BE, THE MORE I SEEM TO EXPERIENCE KINDNESS. IF SOMEONE DOES SOMETHING KIND, I ALWAYS SAY, "THANK YOU, THAT'S KIND." I HOPE THAT BY NOTICING AND NAMING IT THAT I AM HONOURING IT AND ENCOURAGING IT.'

Susie Hills, Founder of Kindfest

Is Humility Innate?

While it's true that some people find that being humble comes naturally to them, it's also, like most things, a trait that can be practised and learned. You may want to increase your levels of generosity to others and hang back from your natural thirst for the spotlight. Whatever the case, the key is practice and later on, we will look at some scripts for developing your humility. Read them aloud to yourself, notice your reactions and how you feel. The scripts are a little like trying on new clothes. Which ones feel 'more you' and which ones are the bold fashion statement that would result in a radical transformation for you?

Julie Nerney is an executive and non-executive director based in the UK. She's taken on big roles in government, as well as turning around large corporations and overseeing the transport strategy for the London 2012 Olympic Games. I asked whether she thought humility could be learned. Julie puts humility very high on her list of desirable traits and told me that self-awareness is key. She listed getting comfortable with asking for honest feedback, using psychometric tools and finding a good coach as her vital self-awareness tools: 'It never fails to amaze me how valuable (and surprising) these insights are. Our own self perceptions are woefully inaccurate. It takes time and effort and needs a real commitment to want to do it. The deeper your self-awareness, the more you realize how much you don't know and the more open to humility you are.'

Be the Spotlight, Not the Star

Genuine humility comes from a desire to support and elevate others and a recognition of the roles that things like teamwork, luck and privilege play in our success, whereas being a pushover comes from a lack of confidence or feelings of intimidation. Being humble is often mistaken for being a pushover, or being too soft, but it requires a level of self-confidence – you have to know that your own talents will be recognized, even if you're not always 'on show' because you are busy helping others to shine.

My friend and Think Productive colleague Grace Marshall calls this 'being the spotlight, not the star'. I love this phrase, because not only are you making a star shine, but you're also still adding your own brilliance.

Lowering Authority to Increase Power

One of the quietest but most powerful acts of kindness I've ever received was when my boss, Max McLoughlin, was talking me through everything I needed to know on my first day in my first proper job at the University of Birmingham. Max had a Word document printed out with a long list of bullet points, everything from safety and contract information to some suggestions for first projects and people to say hello to. The final bullet just said 'I'm harmless'.

When we got to that point on his agenda, we had a reassuring five-minute conversation where he just reiterated that he was happy to have me on the team, that there was no such thing as a stupid question and that he was there to help. Max could have chosen to exert his authority, or make it all about his grand vision – and all about him – but his instinct was to manage through trust and humility.

Those two words left such an impression on me. I carried them in my head for the next three years as I worked for Max and true to his word, his power as a manager was in being relatable, honest and supportive. I worked incredibly hard for him and it had nothing to do with being scared. And because so much of how we learn people-management comes from our early bosses, those two words have been passed on to many others over the years since then.

Witnessing

A great way to be the spotlight and not the star is to put yourself in the role of witness. Witnessing is the art of showing someone just how good the movie of their life is.

Witnessing is a delicate role. It takes empathy and kindness, of course. And practice too. Witnessing is about revelling in a supporting role and rarely about problem-solving or comparing your own stories with theirs, tempting as those reactions are. It doesn't need an answer or an ending. It's not about the future, it's about the now. Witnessing isn't just about the big stuff, either. It's the few words you exchange with a cashier at the supermarket, acknowledging their long shift is nearly over, or the tiny emails that say 'Well observed', or 'Go, You!' or 'I bet you're glad *that's* over'.

I learned a lot about witnessing the day I accompanied my Ugandan friend, Abudu Waiswa Sallam, to his Masters in Law graduation ceremony at Nottingham Trent University. Abudu lives in Kampala and through sheer hard work (and a magnetic personality), his life has been as close to a 'rags-to-riches' story as they come. He was in the UK for a conference, but no one from his family could fly over to attend his graduation, so he was going alone. But what's the point in picking up the certificate if there's no one there to witness you do it? I decided I had to be there.

Ugandans have very high sartorial standards and seem to spend a lot of time polishing their shoes, even though they know that the dust or rainy season mud will ruin them in just a few short hours. That morning, we woke up early and I emerged from my room in a three-piece suit and tie. It was the first time Abudu had ever seen me wearing a suit, but that day it felt important to mark the occasion and signify its importance. I'll never forget the look of pride on his face: 'Eh, man! You look sooo smart!'

We spent hours on the trains to Nottingham and back, putting the world to rights. I took Abudu for his first ever Wagamama meal to celebrate, whooped

and cheered embarrassingly when his name was read out during the graduation ceremony and of course, we posed for some graduation pictures, where
we joked that I was his honorary step-dad for the day. I enjoyed that day more
than I did my own graduation. What a gift it is to bear witness for others.

Exercise: Ego Check

Ego is our sense of self. Self-confidence and self-esteem can help us
hold our nerve when we're pioneering something new, or have the
bravery to put our heads above the parapet and challenge things that
are wrong, or situations where we're wrong – we could call that 'having
a modest ego'.

Quiet confidence is the state of mind that drives results without
letting ego get in the way too much. Whereas, when we veer from
self-confidence to self-importance, and when we get too wrapped up
in worrying about how much we're winning, or how we're perceived
that we head into the uncomfortable territories of 'big ego' and 'fragile
ego' and even 'show-off'. And while many a late night and many a
brilliant idea have been born from insecure people's desires to 'prove
everyone wrong', I think there's a profound sadness to that being the
dominant motivation for someone's success.

We're all guilty of letting our egos get the better of us. Here are a
few ego-check questions. See which ones draw you in and which repel
you. Chances are the ones that elicit strong reactions on either end of
that spectrum are where you might need to spend time:

- Over the last week, can you think of a time where it was more
  important for you to be right than to listen to someone else's view?
- Think about what you're currently working on. Simple question:
  Who is it for?
- Are you more interested in making your parents proud, making
  a contribution or winning? If it's winning, what do you think the
  game is? (And are you sure everyone else is playing?)

- Why did you really post that thing on social media last week, if you're brutally honest with yourself?
- Who needs more of your curiosity and support this coming week?
- How can you be more of a spotlight and less of a star? What would be the consequence of that? And now, how about the benefits of that?

Now that you've reflected on those questions, are there any burning actions for the week ahead?

'THE FUNDAMENTAL CAUSE OF THE TROUBLE IN THE MODERN WORLD TODAY IS THAT THE STUPID ARE COCKSURE WHILE THE INTELLIGENT ARE FULL OF DOUBT.'

Bertrand Russell, Philosopher

Humble Scripts

The following phrases ('scripts') are a great way to practice humility: to give others the space and show the world that there's something more at stake in our work than self-satisfaction.

'I DON'T KNOW...'

The desire to appear the most knowledgeable person in the room can sometimes stop us from asking for advice. 'I don't know' can feel like an admission of weakness. In fact, it's the opposite. It shows that you're comfortable with ambiguity and projects self-confidence. More often than not, saying 'I don't know' is refreshing. We hear it so rarely that when you hear someone whose opinions you respect call out for curiosity, or more data, or more reliable expertise, it reinforces the need to check our egos or else risk them derailing our decision-making altogether.

'WHERE ARE WE STUCK?'

This is truly one of the most powerful questions we can ask and is especially powerful when we make a habit of asking it on a regular basis. It creates the space for the possibility that things do get stuck. It creates psychological safety, because it acknowledges that being stuck isn't a personal failure, it's a natural part of the process of work. And it gives everyone permission to talk about the struggles, so that together, the team can help solve them. Many hands make light work.

The bravado of work often leads us to believe that certain people always know what to do. But the truth is that most of these people are just better at hiding their problem-solving from plain sight, or simply more comfortable dwelling on uncertainty or ambiguity. Creating the safe space to be stuck is halfway to unsticking – until tomorrow when you do it all again.

'I MADE A MISTAKE'

We all desire – perhaps more than anything else in the workplace – to feel that we are productive, conscientious and reliable in our work. We want to feel trusted and valued. So perhaps it's no wonder that we find it so hard to own up when we get it wrong. One of the golden rules of entrepreneurship is that there's no such thing as a failure, only feedback. Mistakes and mis-steps are all part of the process of making things happen and creating change. Trying to hide our mistakes denies others the opportunity to learn from them and creates a culture where everyone else does the same. It's important to role-model vulnerability and an openness to learning and changing if you want others to exhibit these qualities too.

'WHAT ARE WE GRATEFUL FOR?'

Gratitude practice aids humility in a number of different ways. Consistently asking yourself 'what am I grateful for?' has been proved to release oxytocin and boost happiness chemicals in the brain (which, as we learned earlier in Part One, helps build trust too). This simple act of self-kindness boosts feelings of empathy and lowers stress levels.

But when we start to talk about gratitude as a group, the magic really happens. It can be as simple as asking each person at the end of a meeting to share something they have valued, or you can dive a bit deeper and ask them to share their appreciation for something someone else around the table has contributed in the meeting, or done recently. This builds trust, encourages deeper and more vulnerable conversations and of course, everyone likes to hear praise or compliments for things that have gone well, too.

'THAT'S SO KIND OF YOU TO SAY'

Do you have a hard time accepting compliments? It can be all too easy for us to downplay our successes for fear of our egos being too overbearing. Recently, I had an off-mic conversation with one of the guests on my podcast. The guest paid me a huge compliment about my interviewing skills, telling me it felt like a very present, free-flowing conversation. My immediate reaction was to fall into the 'Oh, it was nothing', 'Of COURSE I read the book, it's the least I could do' and 'Well, I was rubbish at the beginning, but I've done nearly 200 episodes so you'd HOPE I'd be good by now…'.

The guest surprised me by asking me if I would like some feedback. He really took me to task on being *too* humble, encouraging me to own the compliments, and pointed out that when someone tells you how great you are, they put themselves in a vulnerable position. By not meeting that with vulnerability of my own, I was doing him a disservice. So now when I get similar comments, I try my best not to deflect. 'That's so kind of you to say', or 'Thank you, that means a lot to me' are much better starting points than 'Well, here's why you're wrong'.

'GOOD CHALLENGE'

This is an important phrase for group dynamics. No one loves being wrong or being challenged, but sometimes a healthy disagreement gets us all to somewhere better – in fact, it's often the only thing that does. I got an email from a colleague who had objected to a decision I was making, explaining the impact that this decision had on their work. The email got my hackles up and I felt defensive. My first instinct was to fight back but after a few deep breaths, I realized that perhaps she was right after all. Rather than trying to justify my position in the reply, I deliberately started my email back with the words 'Good challenge'.

So, 'good challenge' is a phrase that not only offers warmth and connection where otherwise there might be defensiveness, but it also acts as a signifier for the future and sets the tone for others: 'If I'm wrong, I'll listen', 'I'm open to challenge', 'We should all encourage scrutiny of our ideas'. This is one of the kindest ways you can treat healthy disagreements, ensuring that everyone feels safe to raise the difficult stuff that makes a difference.

'CAN YOU HELP ME UNDERSTAND?'

Sometimes we get stuck. Sometimes tension doesn't clear and before we know it, a small disagreement feels like a war. What we know for sure when these moments happen is that they fester unless they're addressed properly. One way to break the ice and get back to a healthier disagreement is to ask the other person if they can help you see it from their point of view. 'Help me understand your thinking here' is a great way to say 'What matters right now is not that I win, but that I understand'. It's generous, kind and yes, often extremely tough to do. But it matters. A word of caution with this one, though: watch out for it being used passive aggressively.

'I'VE THOUGHT ABOUT THIS, AND CHANGED MY MIND'

Everyone loves a bit of decisiveness. But what happens when you've made a decision that, pretty quickly, is beginning to look foolish? Well, as with so many of these scripts, the best thing to do is also one of the hardest things to do. To own up. To admit that you didn't see something coming, or that you acted before you had the right data available. Especially when it comes to political decisions, we view U-turns as wholly negative, but in life, we sometimes need the freedom and space to be able to change our minds. When we've genuinely got something wrong and we start to see that, what can get in the way is our ego and pride. There's no point holding onto a bad decision and digging in just to save embarrassment. Better for the long term to be seen as someone humble enough to recognize the limitations of their thinking and kind enough to limit the damage.

'HOW COULD THIS BE EVEN BETTER?'

The Japanese word 'Kaizen' means 'continuous improvement'. The philosophy of Kaizen has been applied to everything from factory assembly lines – where it encouraged cultures of regular feedback to keep tweaking processes and increase efficiency – to psychotherapy and life coaching, where it's been used as a way of acknowledging that all of us have more to learn.

When we accept that there's always change to make, improvement opportunities to find and an obligation to give and receive feedback, we allow this to exist in a way that's detached from judgement. This approach allows us to stop thinking about ourselves as works of art and instead focus on being comfortable with the idea of being a work in progress, laying the groundwork for what we need to hear, or what we need to change. At the end of meetings, in regular conversations and in supervisions, couching some discussion around the concept of 'even better if' allows for the good aspects of something to be building blocks and bring more challenging feedback to the table in a safer, more comfortable way.

'I AM NEVER SATISFIED THAT I HAVE HANDLED A SUBJECT PROPERLY UNTIL I HAVE CONTRADICTED MYSELF AT LEAST THREE TIMES.'

John Ruskin, Victorian writer, philosopher and polymath

What to Do When Someone Else Lacks Humility

The 'problem' can often be somewhere else – or more accurately, someone's else's big ego. In those circumstances, it can be tempting to try and become as loud or as blow-hard as them, to try and be heard. However, the opposite is more effective. Early on in my career, I was being coached for a job interview process that involved a group problem-solving exercise. My manager Annette, herself one of the most quietly confident and kind leaders I ever worked with, gave me this advice: 'The panel will set the task. What will then happen is the biggest egos in the room will struggle for dominance. Don't engage with it. Hang back, let them flap around and then when it dies down, you strike. What the panel are really looking for is the ones who can listen, summarize and build an emerging consensus. Let them wear themselves out, then quietly show that you're in control.'

I followed Annette's advice, and got the job. But more importantly, I carried her words with me for the next 20 years.

Questions for Reflection

- Can you think of a time in your career when you let your ego get the better of you?
- Which of the 'humble scripts' above do you most think you need to practise?
- Who around you values humility and quiet kindness above noisy egos?

Kindness Challenge: Metta Meditation

This week's challenge takes the form of a loving kindness meditation. I learned Metta meditation after I met a Buddhist monk at the bus stop in Sri Lanka. I'm not religious, but nevertheless have found it to be a powerful technique and spending time at his monastery was a magical experience. There are many studies[3] that point to it reducing anxiety and stress, being a reliever of chronic back pain and even leading to a longer life. I invite you to practice this meditation for a few minutes each day.

Sit comfortably, in whatever way this works for you:

- Close your eyes, or focus on a burning candle or a tree outside.
- Fill the room with silence, or music, or even a guided Metta meditation from YouTube if you like.

Metta meditation is a form of Buddhist prayer. In it, you sit quietly and recite through a process, which starts with you and then moves through other people and things in your life.

STAGE ONE – YOU

'May I be happy. May I be well. May I be peaceful. May I be safe. May I have ease'. (And don't worry here about the exact words, you can change them if you'd like.)

STAGE TWO – YOUR LOVED ONES

'May [insert names] be happy. May they be well. May they be peaceful. May they be safe. May they have ease'.

Then, follow the same process, moving through different areas of your life. However many you skip, or however you get there, I recommend focusing on the last one on the list:

- Neighbours
- Friends
- Animals
- The environment
- Colleagues
- People who are suffering
- My enemies / people who have done me wrong.

Practise this meditation for a few minutes each day. Notice how you feel at the end and any emotions that the process brings up for you. Feelings of anger, frustration and loss can occur, as well as happiness, peace and gratitude.

'IF YOU UNDERSTOOD
EVERYTHING I SAID,
YOU'D BE ME.'

MILES DAVIS, JAZZ TRUMPETER

Graham All

6. Treat People the Way THEY Want to be Treated

Often it is said that you should treat people the way you'd want to be treated. That's a good aspiration for basic-level respect, but what's truly kind is to treat people the way THEY would want to be treated. It means having our impact match our intent. Treating people how they want to be treated means making it kind on both sides.

The worry that our intended kindness might not be received in the right way is surprisingly high. The BBC and University of Sussex's Kindness Test research published in 2022[1] found that the idea of 'kindness being misinterpreted' was the most popular reason people gave as the barrier to their being kind (with 65.9 per cent giving it as their main reason not to take action). We want our intent to be good – to be acting from a place of genuine love and care, and we want the results to bring happiness, not confusion or something worse.

How Do We Make Sure Our Impact is as Good as We Intend?

Of course, sometimes we have to take a little bit of a leap of faith when it comes to acts of kindness. We can make our best guesses, based on how well we know somebody, of what they will appreciate, what they'd see as funny, the constructive criticism or truth they'd be able to stomach versus not, and so on. It's all about increasing the odds that when you take such risks, they pay off. And luckily, kindness and understanding people work in a loop, so the more we practice kindness, the easier it gets.

And How Do We Know That We Hit the Mark? When It's Kind on Both Sides

Of course, the ultimate test of whether impact matched intent is to 'get the data': either to ask the person if they appreciated your actions, or take it from the tears of joy running down their cheeks that you probably did OK. And the more you get to know people, generally the less room there is for error. And while the idea of 'kind on both sides' is useful to help us stop and think about what they want rather than what we think we would want in that situation, we can't hold it up as the definitive measure of whether something is truly kind or not. Sometimes we may do something that we think is exceptionally kind for someone, but they just don't like it, or they are angry with us, or it takes them some time to appreciate it. That said, the idea of our impact matching our intent, and 'kind on both sides', provide us with really useful questions to ask ourselves in the moments when we notice 'the gap'.

I remember one of my first jobs as a manager was welcoming a guy called Eddie to the UK. Eddie had come to us from New York on a year's secondment. This was 2002 and we were fast approaching the first anniversary of 9/11. I remember pulling him into my office to talk about it – I felt it might be a day that would weigh heavily on him. I didn't yet know him well enough to know if any of his friends or relatives had died that day. I remember asking him, 'Do you want us to do anything together to commemorate this anniversary, or would you like some time off?'. Eddie thanked me for asking, but said he'd prefer just to work through as normal on that day. I had visions of us all marking this occasion together, but in the end what he needed was normality.

MAKE IT KIND

INTENTION

IMPACT

ON BOTH SIDES

Getting Curious About People

It's clear that empathetic connection is easier when we can see the whole of a person, not just seeing them through black and white text or as a square on Zoom. When people regularly share an office together, you might call these the 'watercooler moments' but it's clear that in today's hybrid and flexible working culture, we have to make a bit more effort to seize those random moments when work is not the only thing on the agenda. Here are a few ways you can do that:

- Create WhatsApp or Slack groups for following TV shows.
- Arrange an office sweepstake for events like the football World Cup.
- Bring a little bit of the personal into the start of meetings – for example, asking people to share what they're planning on doing over the weekend.
- Give staff a day off or half day off on their birthdays and ask them to share a photo of them enjoying that time.
- If someone mentions their child or partner's birthday is next Tuesday, immediately set an alarm in your phone so that on the day you can send them a quick message.

These little ice-breakers can often lead to five-minute conversations that allow you to really connect with how someone is feeling.

Act With Love

Of course, it's not kind on both sides if your intent was self-centred or passive aggressive. We have to act with love. Love and heart are things that we don't often talk about with regards to work, but they're fundamental in understanding what drives human behaviour at work. Entrepreneurs start companies to follow their passion and do something they love, or because they have a vision for how they can make a dent in humanity. As we develop co-dependent relationships and line managerial relationships at work, we act out of loyalty and concern for those who have shown the same for us, and when serving our customers, we are driven by how we can show them that we care about their needs, or make them feel surprised or delighted.

'I THINK LOVE IS SUCH A MISUNDERSTOOD WORD. WE ASSOCIATE IT SO NARROWLY, WITH ROMANTIC LOVE, WITH FINDING SOMEBODY BEAUTIFUL AND IMPRESSIVE, AND BEING AMAZED BY THEM. THAT'S NOT REALLY LOVE. I MEAN, THERE'S ANOTHER VERSION OF LOVE, WHICH IS REALLY SHOWING CHARITY AND IMAGINATION TOWARDS ANOTHER PERSON. SO, WHEN YOU SEE BAD BEHAVIOUR, YOUR FIRST THOUGHT IS HOW DID THAT PERSON GET THERE? WHAT'S THE CHILD INSIDE THAT PERSON? THAT PERSON WHO'S NOW GNARLED AND ANGRY WAS ONCE A VULNERABLE INFANT. WHAT HAPPENED TO THAT PERSON?'

Alain de Botton, Author

When it comes to hospitality, few places match the opulence and attention to detail of the United Arab Emirates. If you have ever stayed in a hotel in Dubai or Abu Dhabi, or been to a meeting or conference there, you'll know that you're guaranteed a warm welcome. Of course, for emerging cities looking to become major tourism and business destinations, it doesn't hurt to have incredibly high standards when it comes to hotels and restaurants. But there's another reason why the UAE has such a culture of generous and lavish hosting, and it goes back a few generations to when Dubai was a tiny fishing port and its citizens were nomadic Bedouin travellers.

The Bedouin tribes travelled around the Arabian Peninsula for centuries and one of their beliefs was that when they saw another group of travellers approaching their camp, they would make a lot of effort to lay on fantastic hospitality for them. This had an altruistic motivation because it showed friendliness and built rapport, but there was also another very practical reason for rolling out the red carpet. Because water and certain foods were scarce in the desert, the Bedouins were very aware of inter-dependency. That week, they might be the ones who had an abundance of resources and were well-fed, but the following week, they could be the ones on the lookout for what they needed to survive. And when they're in need, if they happen to stumble across a group to whom they have previously given generous hospitality, they can expect the same back, just when they need it most. So, in many ways, a lot of our altruism is also selfish and it reflects the genuine inter-dependencies facing our world.

Find Your Generosity Mindset

Principle One of our Eight Principles of Kindfulness at Work (*see also* page 63) is the idea that 'Kindness Starts With You' and that without self-kindness, it's much harder to be kind to other people. A key part of this self-kindness is choosing to be generous from a mentality of abundance. When I was younger, I dated a chef who earned only a little more than the minimum wage. She never had any money left over at the end of the month, but if she had coins in her pocket and someone needed help, she was always the first to hand them over. At times, she went without. And she *always* survived.

As someone who always worried about money, largely as a result of childhood memories of my parents' money struggles, her example taught me to have an abundance mentality. The world has enough for you, and even when times are hard, it's possible to give generously. Again, this helps create a world where you can occasionally receive generously if you need to, too.

> 'I REALLY WANT TO ENSURE THAT PEOPLE UNDERSTAND THAT, AS A LEADER, I'M NOT JUST THERE IN TITLE-NAME ONLY. I REALLY WANT PEOPLE TO UNDERSTAND THAT I AM INVESTED IN THEM. THE ONLY WAY HONESTLY THAT I THINK I'VE BEEN ABLE TO DO THAT IS JUST THROUGH MY ACTIONS. AS CHEESY AS IT MAY SOUND, I WANT THEM TO GO INTO EVERYTHING AS THE BEST VERSION OF THEMSELVES, AND THE MOST CONFIDENT VERSION OF THEMSELVES AS WELL.'
>
> **Justin Placide, Assistant Director, Department for Business, Energy and Industrial Strategy, UK government**

Inclusive Language

It's important to be serious about honouring difference and diversity in our teams. This is an area that gets unnecessarily politicized, with the idea that 'political correctness has gone too far' and is 'stifling freedom of speech'. The comedian Stewart Lee put it best when he described political correctness as 'an often-clumsy negotiation towards a kind of formally inclusive language', adding, 'There's all sorts of problems with it, but it's better than what we had before.' Kindfulness is about being committed to using language that feels inclusive and avoids prejudice. What's also kind is to give everyone the space to screw up once in a while, without them being hounded or 'cancelled' for it, because none of us are perfect.

Similarly, words or phrases that would carry negative associations or cause offence for certain groups should be avoided, but there is a range and a clumsiness here too. In 2017, Anne Marie Morris, a British Member of Parliament, used the phrase 'n*gger in the woodpile' in a debate. Because it included that word, it should have been obvious to Morris that the phrase was outdated and highly inappropriate (she was suspended by her Party for using it). On the other hand, the word 'brainstorming' has a long history of people trying to replace it with phrases like 'thought showers' because of its perceived offensiveness to people with epilepsy. Often the problem is that there is a fine line between being sensitive to hurting someone else's feelings and being offended on their behalf. A survey by the Epilepsy Society[2] found that overwhelmingly, people with epilepsy were not offended by the word 'brainstorming'. Switching out the word 'brainstorming' is a great example of a 'nice' act but not a 'kind' one. The intention was kind, but it wasn't kind on both sides.

As someone who makes a living from words, I find the constant evolution of language fascinating. This evolution hasn't always been smooth and it's not unreasonable to assume that there will always be mis-steps where the quest for kinder language doesn't quite meet the mark and that people will make mistakes either through a lack of awareness or a moment of thoughtless forgetfulness. Patience and kindness are important as we all clumsily muddle through to something better.

Lots of people (myself included!) become very nervous about the idea of getting these things wrong. After all, no decent person wants to offend others by unintentionally being unkind with something as small as their words. At times when I've been unsure, either about a specific term in conversation, or about how to address someone in terms of things like pronouns, I've found that the kind (and yes, slightly scary and inconvenient) way is to show a little humility and address the truth of the issue, rather than ignore it until the conversation moves on. Sometimes I've been brave enough to say something like 'I'm worried I'm saying the wrong thing here, can you help me out?', and if appropriate, added something like 'Please do pull me up if I get it wrong', or 'Thank you for your patience'. This is about being committed to learning and being committed to both truth and grace, too.

Avoiding Fake Kindness

There may be times when we are tempted to be kind, but for some other reason other than our own generosity. Social media these days is full of 'influencers' giving away money to homeless people or filming themselves as they try to make someone's day. Would they be doing so if the camera wasn't rolling? And if we hold the door open for someone and they appreciate it, is it kind? But if that becomes just the expectation (and it loses its sense of love and heart) – does it stop being a kind thing to do? In reality, there are often multiple motivations for any act of kindness and perhaps the best measure is 'what was most prominent in your heart?'. When kindness feels inauthentic or 'performative' rather than coming from a genuine place, it can often have the opposite effect to that which is desired.

Remembering the Little Details

Often, memorable colleagues or managers are the ones who, even when you haven't seen them for months on end, ask after your child by name, or remember where you were planning to go on holiday the previous year. I aspire to be that person, but there's a major problem: I have a terrible, terrible memory. My friend, the author and entrepreneur Jodie Cook, introduced me to a great way around this: her 'personal CRM'. Whenever she gets off a Zoom call, or finishes up a lunch with someone, she sends a voicenote to herself, summarizing the stuff that 'future Jodie' will want to remember. And then the next time she's about to see that person, she can quickly brief herself for the meeting by recapping the voicenote. When you remember the little details about people, people remember you.

Leading with Integrity

The best way to make sure your intentions are genuinely kind is to start from a place of high standards. When we have integrity, we are kind. And even when we might miss the mark, we are less likely to diminish trust if someone sees that we have genuine integrity.

In the 1990s, Prime Minister John Major's government had been gripped by scandal, with some of his MPs accused of taking 'cash for questions' – a way for the wealthy to buy influence over government policy. Major set up the Committee on Standards in Public Life in 1994, chaired by Lord Nolan. They reported back, outlining seven principles, now commonly known as 'The Nolan Principles', that were deemed to be essential ethical standards for any MP. These same principles have been adopted by local government bodies, charities and some companies in the UK as a way to articulate clearly and explicitly the basic framework of what a public service role should look like. These were:

- Selflessness – Operating solely in the public interest.
- Integrity – All MPs should avoid being put in a position where they are under any obligation to people or organizations that might inappropriately influence their work, and they should never act to gain financial or material benefits for themselves, family or friends.
- Objectivity – Taking decisions fairly and impartially, without discrimination or bias.
- Accountability – Being accountable to the public for all decisions and submitting fully to the required scrutiny.
- Openness – Acting and taking decisions in a transparent manner. Information should not be withheld unless there is a clear and lawful reason for doing so.
- Honesty – Telling the truth.
- Leadership – Actively promoting these principles to others and treating others with respect.

Some of these ideas seem to have gone out of fashion in recent years as certain leaders in business and politics have obviously not lived up to these principles, occasionally making it clear that they will do whatever they want, without the need for a moral compass or standards, and ultimately see their only limitation as 'whatever I can get away with'.

We've all worked with liars, or known liars, in our personal lives. After a while, the lies become too difficult to hide, or even too difficult for the person to keep track of, and then they become that person's downfall. At the end of it all, we can't put a price on reputation and when we look back on our careers and our lives, one of the most important questions of all may be: 'Did I act with integrity?'.

Let's be clear: integrity and caring sometimes means leaving money on the table in the short term. But it also means acting in a way that you feel proud of, that is 'for' the people around you and is in line with the human values that we all hold dear. Again, we have a choice to live in a cut-throat world, or a kind one, and we vote with our feet through our actions, every day, to make that choice.

Ultimately, those who operate without integrity have short careers because quite quickly, it gets harder for people to trust you and harder still for people to do business with you. As James Timpson, CEO of Timpson, told me, 'Being a bastard is great in the short term. In the short term, you're a hero and share-holders love you. In the longer term, you're toast.' Trust and psychological safety rely on a basic level of integrity being upheld and I would argue it's impossible to lack integrity and yet still be thought of as a kind leader.

KINDNESS HERO

KINDNESS HERO: CASE STUDY
BRIAN CHESKY, AIRBNB

Brian Chesky and his team built Airbnb in the face of extreme cynicism. Friends, family and most potential investors thought the idea was stupid: why would you trust someone to stay in your home? And why would anyone prefer to stay in a stranger's home than a hotel?

Chesky and his co-founders built a business based on the human touch, believing at every step of the way in the inherent goodness of humans. It began with the idea of staying in the spare rooms of strangers' houses – an experience more intimate and less sanitized than staying in hotels (and especially useful in cities where all the hotels are fully booked because of a big conference or event). As it grew, fans of the site enjoyed its ability to be the conduit for human connection and uniquely tailored experiences, and Chesky's open and affable leadership style earned him the reputation of being one of tech's good guys.

Airbnb's impressive growth over the last decade was based on a 'network effect': when they grew substantially in one city, the guests would take the idea back to where they lived, talk about it with their friends and then become the next hosts. The network effect catapulted Airbnb to become one of the unicorns of its era, but it also presented the company with a problem: hosting Airbnb guests became so lucrative that people bought up properties that were formerly owner-occupied or long-term tenanted and converted them to dedicated Airbnb rentals, pricing local people out of certain housing markets. Local governments in those cities became concerned and tried to ban Airbnb altogether.

Chesky has faced significant legal battles with cities like Paris, Barcelona and London. Asked how he had approached dealing with the regulatory issues in these cities, he said: 'My first instinct was to fight. In 2010 we staged a political rally. We'd go to New York City – we went to City Hall, we gave people signs and they'd help. But then we realized that's not really the right approach for us. We're a company where people are living together and we're trying to teach people that people are fundamentally good. A company where people live together is not a company that should have a brand of fighting! I mean, the big fear is that people are going to fight in their homes and so on, so we thought "we need to be partners of cities." We wanted cities to know we love them.

'So we decided that, y'know, we're gonna kill them with kindness. In other words, we're gonna show them that we want to be partners. I always had this instinct that if people don't like you, you should never talk to them, but somebody told me this saying, "It's hard to hate somebody up close", so I kind of created this counter-intuitive thing, which is I'll meet everyone that hates me. And the goal isn't to make them not hate me at the end, but you'll hate me less if you get to know me, and I think you'll understand me. That was totally counter-intuitive because I used to have this fear that if I didn't convince them, I thought it would be a bad meeting, and I didn't want to have bad meetings. I wanted to avoid conflict. But we basically had this view that said, "We're going to meet everyone, and the more you hate us, the more we might even be inclined to want to talk to you" because we think that's because of a misunderstanding.

'So we decided to go on a listening tour. I had tons of horrible meetings, but months later, there was a lot less vitriol against Airbnb. People suddenly had an understanding. That really helped a lot.'[3]

Chesky's open and genuinely curious demeanour has helped steer his company through some pretty furious backlash from local lawmakers in recent years. And, of course, it's great business sense too, because it's a much less expensive option than retreating to the bunker of war and letting the lawyers do the fighting in a courtroom.

Questions for Reflection

- How can I encourage my team to become more curious about each other?
- What do I love, at work? (and please don't say 'the hot guy in accounts'). Why do I care about what I do?
- Who do I feel a caring bond with?
- Is there anyone in my team who I really struggle to care for? How can I show love and care, even if I don't particularly like them?

Kindness Challenge: Letters of Appreciation

Write a handwritten note to a colleague, like the ones Emily Chang talked about in her 'Kindness Hero' case study on page 132 (or write it on a dedicated email if that feels more 'you'). Suggested subjects for the letter:

- I'm really grateful for your work on… _____
- Your efforts over the last few months have been amazing. I'm particularly impressed by… _____
- Thank you for caring about… _____
- I know you're struggling with XYZ right now… _____

'SLOW DOWN AND REMEMBER THIS: MOST THINGS MAKE NO DIFFERENCE. BEING BUSY IS A FORM OF LAZINESS – LAZY THINKING, AND INDISCRIMINATE ACTION.'

TIM FERRISS, AUTHOR OF *THE 4-HOUR WORK WEEK*

Graham Allc

7. Slow Down

Slow Makes Kind

You don't calm down by fixing the problem, you fix the problem by calming down.

If you have been following the Kindness Challenges at the end of each chapter of this book, then at some point during this process you will probably have been thinking about speed, busy-ness and their effects on kindness. It's something that perhaps you hardly noticed before, but once you spend some time thinking about kindness or thinking about being less busy, you suddenly see the symbiotic relationship that exists between the two. So in this chapter, we'll look at the 'slow mindset' and how it can help support your efforts to be kind. And of course, we'll break it down into some practical things you can do to help you slow down and make space for more kindness.

The biggest cause of accidental unkindness is busy-ness

When we are busy, we are not present enough to be paying attention to those around us. We fail to see 'the gap' when it presents itself and we miss all kinds of opportunities for kindness. When we are rushing through our lives, we also deny ourselves the time and mental space to process what's happening around us. We don't make the space to be kind to ourselves and we also run the risk of reinforcing all kinds of scarcity mindsets at the expense of feeling abundant.

Lisa Smosarski, editor of *Stylist* magazine, told me about the damage that speed can cause: 'When I think about kindness at work, it often feels like it's the first thing to go when any sort of pressure is applied to someone. We're all so much more overloaded these days, and we're seeing these very high burn-out rates at the moment. And therefore, I think people compromise on putting other people first or making space. Over the years, I've certainly learned that kindness does take some time.'

Kindness does take time. In the BBC Kindness Test research, 57.5 per cent of people said the barrier to them being kinder was that they thought they didn't have enough time.[1] It also takes connection, space, empathy and an abundance mentality. All of these things struggle to be at the forefront of our minds in periods of hamster-wheel busy-ness. While it seems such an odd question, to ask, 'What's the ROI of kindness?', taking time to slow down and encourage kindness to flourish returns its investment exponentially, by creating the trust and psychological safety that drive us forward.

What does it mean to slow down?

When the Canadian journalist Carl Honoré noticed himself speed-reading *Snow White* to his kids and developing what he calls 'the multiple-page turn technique', he realized he had a problem. Why wasn't he savouring the moments when he got to read stories to his children, and why was he racing through his life instead of just living it? It led him to write *In Praise of Slow*,[2] a book that catalyzed 'the slow movement', a global community of people pushing back against the febrile freneticism of modern life, and his 2005 TED Talk, *In Praise of Slowness*[3] on the topic has been viewed in the tens of millions. But Carl is quick to point out that slowing down doesn't mean doing everything slowly.

'In our "fast forward" culture, people assume "slow" means lazy or unproductive – long lie-ins, getting nothing done. But it's not about doing everything slowly. It's about doing things at the right speed. Musicians talk about the "tempo gusto" – the right tempo for each piece of music. And that's what slow gets at: sometimes fast, sometimes slow and then all the different tempos and cadences in between. So, to me, "slow" is a mindset. It's about quality over quantity, and doing everything not as fast as possible, but as well as possible. It's a very simple idea, but a very powerful one in a world hooked on speed.'

Taking this 'slow mindset', we can see that the benefits of slowing down and their enabling effects on kindness are many:

- Slowing down promotes deeper listening and empathy. It's easier to walk in someone's shoes when you take the time to connect more fully.
- In slowing down, we also start to spot the opportunities for kindness. This is particularly important when it comes to tuning into our emotional selves and what we need.
- When we slow down, there's also time to think about the impact of our actions: it's important to imagine what it's like to be 'on the other side of you'.
- And finally, when we slow down, we savour the journey rather than just trying to rush to a destination, which is an act of self-kindness all of its own.

Rethinking Friction

There's a reason why we seem to be moving faster than ever before: it's because the promise of hyper-convenience is an enticing one. We are told that life will be better, that waiting around, or wrinkles, or discomfort will all be removed. And that ultimately, our smoother, easier lives will be easier. Carl Honoré argues this is a false promise as well as an undesirable one: 'That all sounds very sleek and modern and fun. But actually, it's pretty empty. It's superficial, because it's actually moments of friction that bring us life. Friction creates sparks and heat and light. It's in the discomfort that we discover ourselves. That's when we learn and grow. Don't get me wrong – I want my broadband to be frictionless, but in conversation, I want sparks to fly and to sometimes feel a little bit out of my comfort zone.'

> **'YOU SHOULD MEDITATE FOR HALF AN HOUR A DAY, EXCEPT WHEN YOU'RE BUSY... THEN YOU SHOULD MEDITATE FOR AN HOUR A DAY.'**
>
> **Buddhist proverb**

How to Use the 'Slow Mindset' for Yourself

Below are some of my favourite ways to develop and maintain a 'slow mindset'...

CREATING SPACE

You've probably found yourself at some point explaining to a colleague or relative how you're so busy, but that 'everything will calm down in a couple of weeks' time'. We fail to see that as we get closer to this mystical point two weeks in the future, more than likely we'll have said yes to more things and filled that precious space in our calendars with just as many commitments as we have right now. It's not enough to wait for the world to slow down for us as if by magic. If we are serious about slowing down, we need to say no and cut down on commitments or make measurable changes to our lifestyle. One of the ways I think about this is the multitude of ways that we can 'create space': space in our diaries, space in our minds, blank space in which the things we want to be doing can grow into. Often the first step when we want to start something new really should be to put a stop to something else first. Here are some of the best ways to create space:

WIGGLE ROOM

When you look at your diary, do you see any time written in for answering emails, dealing with unexpected emergencies, eating or having chance conversations? Probably not. And yet, when you look at your to-do list for the day, you're still much more likely to think about having seven hours to play with rather than the four or so you have left if you'd actually added all of this to the calendar.

Similarly, when planning agendas for all-day meetings, we tend to schedule in only the discussions that we are expecting, yet leave no time for the conversations that may crop up unannounced. The planning fallacy teaches us that we are forever overestimating how much we can get done and underestimating the time taken up with surprises or day-to-day maintenance tasks. With this in mind, we need to add 'wiggle room' to everything we do.

Recognizing our own inconsistencies around planning is one of the first steps to slowing down. I remember when I worked as a freelancer, I used to submit proposals for particular projects based on an estimated number of days. The first few times I did this, I was always wildly underestimating the number of days involved, which led to the inevitable sense of resentment when I then found myself working days for free to finish the project. A fellow freelancer offered me some life-changing advice: 'Work out how many days you need, then double that figure for the proposal.' Yes, we often underestimate these things not by just a little bit, but to where we need double the time we first thought. This same mindset can be used all over our work in order that we can move through the day feeling unrushed. For meetings I'm chairing, my favourite technique is to include a secret slot near the end of the day where I know that item might only take five minutes, yet it's allotted 20 or 30 minutes. This secret 'stash' of time is there just for me and it's my wiggle room if one of the other items on the agenda runs late, or there's unexpected turbulence.

Wiggle room is also worth thinking about whenever you're making time-based decisions: I always used to be late for everything, but now I add 20 minutes of wiggle room when planning journeys. In my head, I'm sitting at the destination for 20 minutes with little to do, but when it comes to it, that 20 minutes is usually swallowed up along the way as I deal with something unexpected and miraculously, I'm then pretty much on time!

The beauty of wiggle room is that it enables a slower, more confident and more present attitude. The confidence of knowing you're not late, or too busy, and that you're exactly where you should be allows for less rushing and more kindness. And at the same time, because you're adding in the wiggle room, you have to be more decisive and not over-schedule yourself.

PHONES AND HEADSPACE

Our phones fill all the tiny spaces in between things. Where 20 years ago we'd have sat on a train and daydreamed as we gazed out of the window, these days we fill that space with podcasts, messages or games. Of course, it's great that we now have something entertaining to amuse us in the supermarket checkout queue, but in those moments of space – and yes, boredom – our brains often set to work on solving the bigger challenges of the day. Quiet, contemplative reflection time can be extremely valuable and we shouldn't underestimate the cost of losing it. And of course, becoming addicted to constant connection leaves us less able to focus or have the space we need for what author and academic Dr Cal Newport calls 'Deep Work'.

I set aside time every morning that's booked into my calendar, for 'deep work' – where I'm going to quietly and without interruption focus on complex, quality work. Knowing I work best in the mornings, this helps protect my diary when I have the most energy. And again, it means that when I resurface and start plugging myself into the emails and messages, I'm doing so with less anxiety that these messages are 'stealing' my precious time. I see it that the deep work times are set aside for me to do my work and the rest of the time, my job is to help everyone else do theirs. For me, that psychological shift has enabled me to be more present, slower and altogether less self-driven (and more generous) in my interactions.

How much 'deep work' time you need each day will depend largely on your role and of course, this changes over time, but I'd recommend using an app like Freedom to block distracting websites, apps or social media during that heads-down time. If you feel like you're ever too attached to your phone (which, if we're honest, is almost everyone), then you'll see profound benefits by being more intentional about what is allowed or not allowed to have your attention at different times of the day.

IT'S NEVER A BAD IDEA TO GO FOR A WALK

We all know that walking is great for our mental health so why is it that times of intense stress are also the times when we tell ourselves, 'I don't have time to go for a walk'? I'm particularly bad at denying myself what I need when I'm busy, but I can honestly say that I've never come back from a short walk around the park and regretted making the time for it.

Walking helps us to feel more present, gives us a sense of perspective and helps us reconnect with our bodies, which in turn reduces stress. When I walk, I also try to slow down the pace of my walk. To feel good – not guilty – about stopping for a few minutes to sit on a bench, or pick some blackberries. Walking is a reset for the brain.

The Japanese word 'shinrin-yoku' means 'forest bathing'. For thousands of years, the Japanese have known what science is now proving: that being among trees and nature aids our breathing and is good for our mental health. Walking is a great way to slow us down and as we wander, our minds wander to those around us: Who needs some help? What did we hear today that we didn't quite process? What ideas do we have to move things along? When I feel guilty about taking time out for a walk, I remind myself that regular walks should be on the job description of every creative and every leader.

THE POWER OF THE PAUSE

My friend Sally-Anne Airey was the first working mother to be a Commander in the Royal Navy. She has a unique perspective on leadership, strongly valuing decisiveness as you might expect, but also mindfulness, embodiment and presence. One of the things she teaches is 'the power of the pause' – taking a moment to breathe, connect with your body and set clear intentions. Pauses realign us with our intentions and slowing down is the difference between decisiveness and impulsive or reactionary behaviour. There are a number of ways that we can invoke the power of the pause to help us slow down, connect and be kinder.

The Preparedness Mindset

We've all been in the kind of situations before where we haven't had the time to do the reading before a meeting, or taken the time to do the thinking or preparation that someone has asked for before a conversation. Often, for fear of looking unprofessional or under-prepared, we try to nod along through the meeting, or 'fly by the seat of our pants', rather than admit to being less prepared than we should be. This comes from a place of self-preservation, but it's deeply disrespectful and actually unkind.

Preparedness is a necessary part of our work, but it's not a part that gets rewarded. It's much less interesting than being in the thick of the action and if we're not careful, the work of being prepared is something we don't think about too much until there isn't enough time left for it, so here are a couple of things that can help you to slow down, which will have the added benefit of giving more attention and respect to the people you're working with.

WEEKLY AND DAILY REVIEW

I've never been a naturally organized person and always found the idea of preparedness a bit dull, but over the last few years, one of the most important parts of my working week is the couple of hours I spend in 'Review' mode. I have a checklist, where I go through things like…

- What meetings have I had over the last week? What follow-up is needed from each one?
- Day by day, appointment by appointment, what's happening over the next two to three weeks?
- What travel plans do I need to make?
- Project by project, what's coming up? What am I behind on? What actions are needed?
- When will I go running?
- How's everybody doing?

It's a couple of hours of deep thinking, reflection and planning that enables me to feel fully in control. I might be overloaded, but I'm not overwhelmed. The benefit of this time is that it helps keep me much more proactive than reactive and stops me from spending all my time in 'brainless and busy' mode. And because it helps me realize exactly how much is already on my plate, it slows me down and keeps me grounded.

I do a tiny version of the same thing at the start of every day (ideally, it's best done before you open your emails, although that's always tempting!). These checklists and rituals keep me on track and stop me from feeling stressed, which means I'm kinder, but are also a great way to spend some time reflecting on what I've achieved (which I rarely do otherwise), so it's a ritual of self-kindness too.

CHECKING IN

When we slow down and have the time to think ahead, there's a tendency to also think about what's coming up for everyone else around us. When that happens, the trick is to act on it. This can be as simple as remembering when you see a colleague across the corridor to ask, 'Are you all prepped for next week's event?' or just firing off a quick text to say 'I'm thinking of you. Go smash it!'. Tiny check-ins can make a big difference. What I find is that many of these check-ins don't really lead to a long or deep conversation, but every now and again, they act as the little warning flag that someone *isn't* ready, they're not coping and they need a bit of help, so you can also view these check-ins as a little bit of a temperature check to gauge stress levels and where project progress is likely to be. I'm generally a really forgetful person, so if I hear someone talking about a big personal thing that's coming up, I'll usually make a note on the top of my calendar, so that morning, it flashes up a reminder for me to check in with them.

'IF YOU WANT TO GO FAST, GO ALONE.

IF YOU WANT TO GO FAR, GO TOGETHER.'

African proverb

KINDNESS HERO: CASE STUDY
JULIAN RICHER, FOUNDER, RICHER SOUNDS

Julian Richer is the founder of Richer Sounds and, by rights, he should be as busy as anyone else featured in this book. But what's remarkable about Julian is that he still makes time, every week, to listen to what's going on for his people.

Julian turned his love of music and HiFi systems into one of the UK's most successful retail businesses. Richer has a number of mantras that set out a distinctive and dynamic culture. His use of short and regular feedback in the form of weekly staff happiness surveys allows him to take a snapshot of company morale and he takes great care to make sure all of his staff feel looked after.

'The most important thing I think we do, which is different from a lot of companies, is that we're really loyal to our people so we only promote from within. I get a colleague care report, every Friday night, I have every single problem that HR are aware of, where the colleagues are ill or their family members are ill or they've had a bereavement, or they've got mental health issues, or having counselling, or they're waiting for an operation. I get that every Friday night and I often pick up the phone to colleagues and see how they're getting on and track problems. And we often pay for private healthcare, so they don't have to get stressed waiting two years for an appointment and so on. So, kindness is many things.'

Julian told me that shortly after starting his business, in 1982, he had read *In Search of Excellence*[4] by Tom Peters and Rob Waterman, which had had a big impact on his approach: 'They analyzed the most successful companies in the States and the only things they all had in common, these successful businesses from all different sectors, were their treatment of people and their treatment of their customers. That had a big effect on me. And then when I worked very closely with Archie Norman in the 1990s on his turnaround of Asda, I saw that the same things I'd done in my little business worked just the same as in his big business. It's all about how to get the best out of people.'

Richer Sounds' philosophy of treating people well also extends to customers. They seek regular feedback from customers, both online and via the 'we're listening' postcards that are left at the till, and their 'Richer VIPs' scheme ensures that it's the customers who are most loyal who get the best discounts and special offers. Julian is also very careful to do business in the most transparent way possible and to focus on building long-term relationships: 'I want customers to understand the details of what is on offer. If a customer can't find what they want in one of our shops, or aren't completely sure about the suitability of what is on offer, then I don't want to make a sale. Our trading philosophy as well as our incentive scheme is based on that principle. I always say to our sales colleagues that achieving an immediate profit by persuading a customer to buy something that isn't right for them is both wrong and crazy. We should be aiming to keep a customer for life, not for one transaction.'

When Julian turned 60, and started to think about what should happen to Richer Sounds, he created an employee ownership trust and transferred 60 per cent of his shares to his staff. Staff also received bonuses to reward their service, with £1,000 allocated to each year of service. I asked him what he thought he'd learned from the process, a couple of years down the line.

'I think it was a fantastic thing to do to secure the success of the business without having to float and without having to do a sale to a venture capital firm, who would no doubt change the culture. And morale has gone through the roof. Customers seem to like it very much. And yes, I think it definitely has improved employee engagement. But of course, you would have to speak to my people yourself privately and see what they have to say! But I do feel morale is generally pretty good. I mean, I hope it was good before we did that. But I'd like to think we've got wonderful people who did appreciate that change.'

Julian is still involved in the day-to-day running of the business, but has also turned his attention to advocating for a more caring form of capitalism to become the norm, with his books like *The Ethical Capitalist*[5] and *The Richer Way*,[6] as well as being involved in initiatives such as Taxwatch, Zero Hours Justice, the Good Business Charter and the Fairness Foundation.

'I think you have to be holistic about kindness. It's like you hear about these businesses talking about what they do in the community and then you find out they're not paying any tax. There's too much bullshit and greenwashing going on, where you hear businesses projecting themselves as wonderful and then realize that they're using children in the factories that make their products. Kindness has got to be consistent and holistic to have credibility.'

> 'SLOWNESS IS THE MIDWIFE OF KINDNESS. TO BE
> KINDER, YOU'VE GOT TO SLOW DOWN FIRST.'
>
> **Carl Honoré, Author of *In Praise of Slow***

Role-modelling Slow and Creating 'Slow Culture' at Work

Busy-ness often comes from fear. Whenever I've asked a group of people from across an organization about how long is acceptable to leave emails or messages unread, what I find is the more senior you are in the organization, the more relaxed you seem to be about leaving messages for an hour, or two, or even seven. It's the more junior people in an organization who worry about the consequences of small delays. This is often because such things aren't made clear. Everyone operates on assumptions rather than having these kinds of conversations about etiquette and speed out in the open. It's important to role-model slow and intentional rather than quick and impulsive for those around us. It's about reassurance: 'It's OK to clock off, sleep on it, and let's deal with it tomorrow', 'You're doing great, don't feel the need to take on too much', and so on. There are many ways to approach this, so here are a few thoughts and tips and tricks on how to create a culture based on purposeful intentions, not hasty busy-ness.

DON'T BE AFRAID OF RULES AND STRUCTURE

People might assume that the 'nice' way to approach culture is to let everyone do whatever they like, all of the time. But this is a classic people-pleasing mistake because ultimately, it just causes stress and uncertainty. There are also some real benefits to be found in a collective cadence and rhythm to things. Everyone has the mantra of 'don't micro-manage' drummed into them when they first take on management responsibilities and this is of course useful advice, but it's often slightly misinterpreted so that people think it means 'don't impose my ways on others'. However, there are plenty of situations where people are crying out for structure and clarity.

MEETINGS-FREE DAYS

One way of imposing a structure that promotes a slower, kinder working envi-ronment is to bring in some limits on meetings. The most obvious is to allocate a day of the week as a 'no-meeting day'. At Think Productive, we've avoided meetings on Wednesdays for quite a while. This allows everyone some time to work on their own schedule, without feeling pushed around by their calendars. It helps create a bit of scarcity too, which has an added bonus of encouraging a bit more critical thinking before people just try to solve every problem with 'I know, I'll schedule a meeting'.

Also helpful are other approaches, like saying 'no meetings EVER before 11 a.m.' or 'no meetings outside of these core hours'. These small ground rules can have a huge knock-on effect as they help recognize the 'pain point' of meetings and keep consideration for others on your mind before you send out that next big meeting request.

NO-AGENDA LUNCHES

One of the things that speeds up our culture is the sense that we have to squeeze productivity from every moment. Taking the time simply to break bread with a colleague or team, with no agenda or purpose, is a great way to get a tempera-ture check and see how people are feeling. This is of course easier done when you work in the same building, but lunchtime on Zoom is much more pleasur-able than meetings on Zoom.

RENEGOTIATING COMMITMENTS

One of the hardest things for most people is renegotiating commitments. We are taught from childhood that when you say you're going to do something, your word is your bond. This is of course true to some extent when it comes to our work: we want to be reliable and trustworthy team members. But where this falls down is where either an individual or a team takes on a project that seemed important at the time, but pretty quickly or over time, it loses its impor-tance. In these situations, the temptation – often subliminally – is just to carry on: 'I'm committed to this so let's carry on'. Perhaps that person also has some emotional sunk cost investment in carrying on, too. But it's helpful to be the person saying, 'Is this still needed?', 'Can we move this back?', or even 'How can we scale this down and simplify it?'. It's worth remembering that productivity comes from doing less, not more: and focusing on doing the right things, not trying to do everything.

MBWA

Management By Walking Around is something I've seen many effective senior leaders do. It's a great way to build rapport, as well as to see what's happening around the office. The best leaders are those that either take a notebook, or write down actions and follow up straight away afterwards. But it's also a way to instil more kindness and humanity to your leadership, too. Importantly, it also demonstrates that your own diary isn't 'back-to-back-to-back' and that you have time for people. For this reason alone, it helps to slow the culture down.

ROLE-MODEL SLOW

Of course, culture takes its lead from those with influence and power, so use yours to reinforce the good and call out the bad. Tell people about your full lunch break, try to avoid sending emails out of hours unless there's a clear reason or exception (and don't forget you can set your email account to 'work offline', so that you do the work during your evening, but it lands in their inboxes the next morning).

And who needs you as a role-model the most? It's you! So, use this as an opportunity for self-kindness too: go for a walk with no plan, leave your phone in another room (or at home when you go out), spend more time curled up with a good book, practice slow cooking and slow eating, savour the journeys as much as the destinations.

Questions for Reflection

- What bullshit stories do I tell myself about why I'm so busy (and if your first thought is 'No! I'm special! I have reasons I'm this busy right now!', then you need to spend longer contemplating this question).
- What am I going to do to slow down?
- How can I create a culture of slow and intentional productivity, rather than perpetuating the ideas of frenetic busy-ness?

Kindness Challenge: Doing Nothing

What could sound easier? But trust me, you might find this one to be the most difficult challenge of them all. Also, don't tell your boss or significant other that you're doing this one as they'll say you're 'dossing'.

Go to a coffee shop, park bench, or favourite spot. Sit there for at least an hour with no phone, nothing to write with and no other distractions. Notice in that time as you sit there, the stages your mind goes through. You may experience frustration, boredom, restlessness and even feelings of anger or self-loathing. Observe the strangers walking past. What are they doing? Where are they going? What do they need today? Notice how, as your mind slows down, your capacity for kindness increases.

'EVERY MINUTE OF EVERY
HOUR OF EVERY DAY YOU ARE
MAKING THE WORLD, JUST AS
YOU ARE MAKING YOURSELF,
AND YOU MIGHT AS WELL DO
IT WITH GENEROSITY AND
KINDNESS AND STYLE.'

REBECCA SOLNIT, AUTHOR, HISTORIAN AND ACTIVIST

Graham Allco

8. It Doesn't End With You

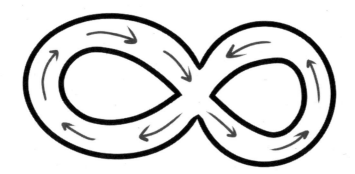

Kindfulness is about being aware of the power of kindness beyond ourselves. It means being a 'culture builder' and helping to set the conditions where people feel they have the permission to act with kindness – creating those 'vessels for kindness' so that they can jump into 'the gap' and take action. When we do this outside of our organizations too, kindness has the chance to work its magic across our society as well.

It is not enough for us to personally think kind and act kindly – we have a duty to make kindness the default response in our organizations and more widely. If Principle One ('Kindness Starts With You') seemed in any way selfish or self-indulgent, then Principle Eight is where we turn that on its head: our own kindness pales into insignificance when set against the idea of infinite loops of kindness.

Being a Culture Builder

A popular definition of culture is, 'the ideas, customs and social behaviours of a particular people or society'.[1] And organizational culture consultancy Gotham Culture defines organizational culture as 'the underlying beliefs, assumptions, values and ways of interacting that contribute to the unique social and psychological environments of an organization'.[2]

PERPETUATING KINDNESS

There are some less-formal definitions of culture that I find helpful. One is to think of culture as 'the way we do things around here' and for leaders to think of it as 'what happens when you're out of the room'. But how can we make sure we embed kindness so that it just becomes the default? Here, we are going to look at the things you can do to ensure that the influence of your kindness is felt as widely as possible: how you help *other people* to spot the gaps for action, how you help them to develop their empathy and trust and ultimately, how you can provide the inspiration for others to develop Kindfulness too.

'TO ME, CULTURE IS A FEELING. IT INCORPORATES A SENSE OF BELONGING. WHEN I JOINED MY CURRENT FIRM, THE CULTURE WAS DEFINITELY DIFFERENT TO MY PREVIOUS PLACE OF EMPLOYMENT. PEOPLE HERE ARE FRIENDLIER, APPROACHABLE, INTERESTED IN FINDING OUT MORE ABOUT YOU, HAPPY, WELL CONNECTED WITH EACH OTHER INTERNALLY. IT SEEMED EVERYONE KNEW EVERYONE.'

Vekria Devila, Learning & Development Specialist, Mayer Brown

Components of Culture

What makes up a culture? There is no one set definition, but here's what I see as the main components , along with some thoughts on how kindfulness can be incorporated:

- Language – how our words, phrases and questions set the tone for the way we think and the way we value others.
- Communication – how different styles of communication and different tools can aid or hinder kind interactions.

- Stories and storytelling – how we can add stories of kindness to the collection of 'folk tales' that get passed from person to person, department to department.
- Ceremonies, rituals and rhythm – how we mark the right moments, to be a witness for people's lives and work.
- Meetings – how things get discussed, how people are treated and how people express themselves and solve problems.
- Attitude to conflict – how having a healthy attitude to conflict is kind.
- How mistakes are handled – how to learn with psychological safety.

Our focus will be mostly on things from the latter half of this list (having covered a lot about language and communication in earlier chapters). First, we'll look at what to do, day-to-day, when times are good. Then we'll look at where kindness really comes into its own: in the darker moments when your organization is in crisis, or you have to deal with awkward or difficult stuff. In many ways, the real test of culture is how it all holds up in the middle of the storm – and the key to getting that right is to make sure the architecture of kindness is in place before the dark clouds gather.

Who are Your Cultural Architects?

When Sven-Göran Eriksson became the manager of the England football team in 2001, it's fair to say he had his work cut out for him. Despite having talented players, the team had under-achieved for many years. The players were idolized by their clubs' fans and most of the team played in the newly-minted Premier League, with TV revenues making millionaires of even the youngest of stars.

These same highly-paid players then had to go and play for their country, which often meant giving up their summer holidays or rest time, while also facing ridicule from the press and being booed and disrespected by the England fans. A lot of the players had stopped taking England duty that seriously. Eriksson knew that he had to change the culture. He had to set high standards and build belief that matched their talent; he had to eliminate the fear of failure and the sense of inevitability that had dominated the culture of the team. And more than that, he knew that it couldn't all be about him.

Eriksson hired the sports psychologist Willi Railo to help. Together, they talked about the concept of 'cultural architects'. Cultural architects are people with high levels of self-confidence and influence, who share your vision for the culture. No football manager can kick the ball on the pitch during the game and only the most charismatic are able to inspire complete mental shifts and five-star performances just with the power of their words alone.

Shortly after taking over as manager, Eriksson identified his main cultural architect and made him the captain of the team. A young David Beckham became the blueprint for what Sven was trying to create: naturally talented of course, but also fiercely ambitious, without fear and conscientiously hard-working. Beckham wasn't there just to uphold a standard, he was there to raise the bar higher. The team flourished, beating Germany 5–1 – a result that even England's players would have said was impossible just a few years earlier.

Willi Railo[3] described cultural architects as 'people that are able to change the mindsets of other people. They're able to break barriers, they have visions, they are self-confident and they are able to transfer their own self-confidence to a group of people. Not more than 5–10 per cent of people are cultural architects, so you can see in one training session and in one match together, you can spot those easily.'

Changing culture starts not with a massive to-do list of things we have to fix or change, but with the notion that we need to find our fellow travellers first. Finding your small 'tribe' of like-minded people makes it much easier to create momentum.

Hiring for Kind

I've lost count of the number of people over the years who have told me a version of the mantra 'Hire for attitude, the rest you can teach'. As we discussed earlier in Part Two, there's no such thing as a 'kind person' or an 'unkind person', and empathy is something that can be developed and taught. But all that said, there will be people with a very high natural ability to spot 'the gap' for kindness (and take the bold action) in any given situation.

Looking for clues on a CV, like regular volunteering work or charity fundraising, or simply a very people-first or human-centred attitude shining out of the covering letter or application, can be a great way to bring people with a high propensity for kindness to the table. In interviews too, there should be plenty of opportunity to find out more about their approach to people and check for an abundance mentality. Indeed, the Eight Principles of Kindfulness at Work would make an excellent checklist to ensure that candidates have the capacity to be kindness heroes.

A CEO of a charity that I used to work with had a fantastic formula for how she built high-performing teams: 'Make sure you've got some wise experienced heads to guide it, some people with lots of energy to fuel it and then make sure there's lots of kindness to hold it all together.'

Removing the Barriers to Kindness

It's worth being aware that some people face more barriers to being kind than others. Gently removing these barriers for people is the essence of Kindfulness and is a great way to unlock untold kindness potential in your existing team.

GENDER AND KINDNESS

In many ways, the 'business bastard' narrative is driven by the idea of the 'alpha male'. When I teach Kindfulness at Work, gender often becomes an interesting discussion. For many men, some of the more emotional or empathetic strands of kindness can be challenging: they might find the idea of kindness too 'soft' or 'feminine', or be hard-wired by the 'business bastard' narratives that have dominated our culture for so long.

Women are found to be naturally more empathetic and so Kindful forms of leadership feel like second nature to many of them. However, for decades, women have been taught, through books like *Nice Girls Don't Get the Corner Office* by Lois P. Frankel,[4] that the way to succeed at work is to behave in a more 'alpha male' way. In essence, 'Fit in with the men, play it their way and you're more likely to win'. Perhaps we need to reverse the narrative. The future of work will see a greater emphasis on 'people skills' or 'soft skills', and the emphasis on kindness will continue to grow. So, instead of women 'being more like the guys', perhaps the future for us all should be 'Be More Jacinda'.

INTROVERSION AND KINDNESS

You may be surprised to learn that although I'm a regular keynote speaker and someone who makes a living by 'putting myself out there', I'm also an introvert. The BBC Kindness Test[5] of 2021/22 found that more naturally extrovert personalities have a greater tendency towards kindness than introverts do. Whereas introverts look inwards for energy, extroverts gain theirs from other people and hence they are not only more in tune with people, but will tend also to spend more time in the company of others.

But that doesn't mean that introverts are unkind, just that the quiet power of kindness tends to be even quieter and more discrete with introverts: I am much happier, for example, praising someone's work on email or in a 1-2-1 conversation than I am making a speech and asking a room to give that person a round of applause – and likewise, *receiving* praise or applause in front of others is a moment of high anxiety, not a moment of glory for me. Introverts can also have a harder time asserting themselves in a group and so the distinction between 'nice' and 'kind' is particularly important for them and just being aware that in a loud culture where there is competition to be heard, the kindest thing you can do is to remember that introverts need space to shine.

PEOPLE ARE KINDER WHEN THEY FEEL INCLUDED

Some people will feel included and invested in a Kindful culture without you having to try very hard. This could be because they are extrovert, but also because nothing in their appearance or character or background stands out from the majority of the team. But what if you're 20 years older than everyone else, or the only team member with brown skin, or the only person with those religious beliefs, or the only person of your gender or sexuality? Celebrating difference is vital for a sense of inclusion and once people feel included, they find it easier to express kindness, in their own unique way, which adds to the richness of the experience for everybody.

'WHO HAS A VOICE AND INFLUENCE? WHO IS
ACKNOWLEDGED, INCLUDED, CONSIDERED,
INVITED TO THE PUB AND SO ON? THERE
IS A KINDNESS IN INCLUSION, A BRAVERY
IN ACKNOWLEDGING ONE'S OWN PRIVILEGE
AND THAT ALL CONTRIBUTES TO AN
ORGANIZATION'S CULTURE.'

Juliet Flynn, Organizational Development Consultant,
Canterbury Christchurch University

Kinder Meetings

Nothing tells you more about an organization's culture than the way it handles meetings. And while there are plenty of meetings that really should have just been an email instead, great meetings can be the catalyst to all kinds of wonderful results, as well as deeper mutual understanding.

Your role should be to chair (when it's your meeting) or steer (when it's not) each meeting so that it's a space for respectful dialogue, healthy tension and creative spark. Productive meetings focus on action and are full of truth and grace. Here are some ways that you can create deeper spaces for listening in every single meeting you're involved in (and if you're not doing this, you should be questioning their reason for happening!).

START WITH A CLARITY OF PURPOSE

When you invite people to a meeting, they should arrive with clear expectations. Make sure there's an agenda (a list of the substantive items for discussion) as well as a purpose statement. The purpose statement should answer the question 'how will we know when we've finished?'. Purpose statements can transform mediocre meetings.

Here is an example. By the end of this meeting, we will:

- have agreed the timescale and main deliverables for the conference
- have come up with a new name for the conference, or agreed the deadline and process to find one; and
- have decided on project leads and rough budget costs.

Then, the agenda might go into more detail about the order of business, context and issues, strategic choices and the format that each discussion will take. A good tip here is to articulate these as questions (e.g. 'Brainstorm on names: should we use the old name? If not, what new name will fit well with our new strategy to be more topical?', or 'A five-minute presentation from Nathan reporting back on the focus group about the name and then brainstorm on "are we happy with their suggestion, or not?"').

THE OPENING ROUND: BEGIN WITH A POSITIVE REALITY

Nancy Kline's book, *Time to Think*, introduces the idea of an Opening Round. The idea is that at the start of every meeting, everyone is invited to speak. My standard opening round is 'Say your name, how you're feeling right now and one thing that's going well'. (Kline argues that by 'beginning with a positive reality', it sets the tone for positive discussion, too.)

The Opening Round technique is as powerful as it is simple. It ensures that every person in the room speaks, uninterrupted, at the beginning of the meeting, meaning they've 'warmed up' and arrived. In this way it creates an immediate psychological safety because it means someone is never put in the position of sharing a thought that's too risky or contentious without already having spoken (and 'breaking the seal' by at least saying their name means that psychologically, they feel more included in the process of the meeting at that moment). It introduces each person around the table as equal, regardless of status or hierarchy, with everyone getting the same 'airtime'. And it bonds the group together in that moment – important even when you all know each other well.

THE 40-20-40 RULE

When it comes to meetings, remember the 40-20-40 Rule. The idea is that 40 per cent of the attention spent on a meeting should be on preparation, then 20 per cent is spent on the meeting itself, with the final 40 per cent spent on the follow-through of actions. Of course, when we're in back-to-back meetings for days on end, it looks more like the 1-98-1 Rule and so this mindset helps us understand that it's important to be intentional, commit to fewer meetings, but then have better-quality ones. In doing so, we feel under less pressure to rush and are able to take the time we need to listen properly and make the space for kindness.

ELEPHANTS AND UNDERCURRENTS: BRING THE TRUTH, BUT WITH GRACE

Martin Farrell has spent the last 30-odd years as an expert facilitator, working with organizations all over the world, including the United Nations, the Red Cross and the UK government. He helps people to set strategy, make sense of complexity and plan difficult projects. One of the things Martin is very good at is teasing out the things that are difficult to hear. Perhaps there's someone who is fearful that the changes being proposed during a discussion might reduce their influence or even make their job redundant. Maybe there's an idea for a new initiative that rakes up some painful old conversations.

Martin's view is that as a facilitator – the leader of that meeting – you have to be courageous. If there's an elephant in the room, don't let people just dance around it. If there are undercurrents, or conversations that seem to be happening in an underhand way under the table, then, with care, it's your job as facilitator to bring them out from under the table into daylight. It's all about truth and grace.

'There was one particular meeting I was asked to facilitate. There was a guy there who had had control of a particular initiative for many years. It was obvi-ous that the feeling from everyone else there was that this guy was controlling this whole area of work and, by holding onto it, he was holding everything else back. It needed to change and everyone in the room knew it, except him. But no one would speak up. They respected him and were just being too nice. It was a difficult thing for anyone to say to him,' Martin told me.

'I was watching the faces of the leadership team and I could see they were desperate to have this conversation, but no one would break rank. As the clock ticked down towards the end of the meeting, I knew it was my job to be courageous so I asked some incisive questions which opened the way for one member of the group to step forward. I found it hard – in the moment being courageous is not easy. But of course, once the first person had spoken it was much safer for everyone else to chip in and be second to say it. By the end, it was obvious how important it had been to make a change. With the hot topic out in the open, I suggested a small group sit together to work out what needed to be done next. I felt relieved and my client was happy.'

Sometimes your job as the leader of the meeting is to make it comfortable and sometimes your job is to hold people's feet to the fire. Either way, people can only listen to the things that are actually spoken about.

Ceremony, Rituals and Rhythm

'It's the end of the financial year and spirits are in the sky,' says the deadpan accountant Keith, who for one night only is transformed into the role of DJ at the staff party in Ricky Gervais' and Stephen Merchant's classic BBC sitcom, *The Office*. Ceremonies and rituals help to set the rhythm for corporate life, even if some of them feel as frivolous or tenuous as this end-of-financial-year disco. These can be lavish award ceremonies or team off-sites, but can also be moments on Zoom as part of another meeting, or just simple acts of kindness that are shared with the team. Let's look at some of the ways ritual and cere-monies are best used to encourage the right kind of culture.

CELEBRATING ACHIEVEMENTS

- 'Employee of the Week'. This can be included in a team meeting or as an email sent every Friday.
- Ringing a physical (or digital) bell when targets are hit – at Think Productive, our Customer Relationship Management (CRM) sends

out a 'Ding! Ding!' to celebrate new clients joining us, congratulating whoever was responsible for the sale.

- Regular 'Wins of the Week' focus on a Friday, which can be presented by the heads of each department at a meeting, or completed by everyone on email or Slack/Teams.

BUILDING TEAM RELATIONSHIPS

- Start each meeting by encouraging everyone to share something from their lives; it could be what they did at the weekend or something they're struggling with.
- Be aware of religious holidays from all faiths.
- Create spaces to share creativity; i.e. for best cake recipe or best holiday photograph.

ENCOURAGING KINDNESS

- A kindness challenge, where everyone undertakes random acts of kindness for each other, or for customers.
- Split into pairs and everyone is asked to make some kind observations about their partner.
- Kindness awards to recognize the kind acts of colleagues, Timpson-style (*see also* page 200).

SIGNIFYING CHANGE

- Launch parties for new products, in which the people responsible for the launch can be properly thanked.
- Wrap-up parties at the end of projects.
- 'Mourning' or 'reminiscing' parties to remember former colleagues, or former parts of the business that people have an emotional attachment to (I once worked with a couple of charities that were merged into larger entities and the opportunity to formally mark the change was a useful way for people to process the changes and move on).

These rituals and ceremonies are just some of the ways we can kindly create the right rhythm in a culture, but they are not the only ones. It's also worth looking at quarterly cycles, or fortnightly sprints, as well as marking particular parts of the year that may have significance for your organization. (The UK hospitality industry is known for its lavish January parties to celebrate the efforts of staff over the Christmas holidays – this ends up being an important moment to look forward to in what is otherwise a very quiet and uninspiring part of the year.)

Stories and Story-telling

In the 1970s, James March, Professor Emeritus at Stanford University, described leadership as being about striking a balance between being a poet and a plumber. Leaders needed to take care of the plumbing – the organizational systems, the hard information and have a firm grasp of the operational issues – but they also needed to be poets, able to use their words and creativity to capture the imaginations of those working for them. Since then, the number of mediums we have available to us in order to tell stories has increased exponentially, as has the sense of transparency and the pace at which people expect reaction and direction from their leaders.

We talked in Part One about how simply observing acts of kindness can spark very real changes in brain chemistry and promote a sense of motivation, belonging and psychological safety (*see also* page 13). And we know that kindness perpetuates: the more we hear about kindness, the more it ripples through the culture.

Thom Elliot is the co-founder of Pizza Pilgrims, one of the fastest-growing restaurant chains in the UK. He told me about how he encourages everyone across the business to be kind, but also to share their stories of kindness with each other. At Pizza Pilgrims they call this 'Super Kind Bombs'. Staff are empowered and encouraged to undertake small but powerful acts of kindness for each other, but also for customers and partners. It might be creating new pizzas and sharing them with the team, or using their kitchen to teach pizza-making to one of their suppliers' staff, or organizing drawing competitions on the back of their blank pizza boxes. These small acts of kindness are shared with the rest of the organization, which lifts everybody's morale and sets the tone for what's possible.

'THE SMALL THINGS ACTUALLY ARE THE BIG THINGS – BECAUSE THAT'S WHAT CREATES A CULTURE OF KINDNESS.'

Professor Robin Banerjee, University of Sussex Centre for Research on Kindness

---

Eight Ways to Perpetu-*eight* Kindness in Your Culture

There are so many ways that we can drip-feed kind acts into the culture of an organization when times are good. These small things add up and become a powerful signifier of the value of kindness ready for the bad times, when it's so vital. But here are eight other quick ways to perpetu-eight kindness.

1 **Appreciate people and effort, not just results** – This is especially important when people can't control the results. For example, if everyone has worked hard on a tender process or award application, then be the one who reminds them that the commitment was high and that there's things to learn from it. All is not lost. And if someone makes an important contribution to a meeting, or holds respectful disagreement with those around them, then kind words can reassure, as well as set the cultural tone.

2 **Warm Welcomes** – When I visited the offices of I AM Productions, a B2B media agency, they had my name up in lights. There was a light box in reception that said, 'Welcome Graham Allcott'. It's a small thing, but welcoming well shows thought and care and puts people at ease. Putting flowers in a room, giving someone the Wi-Fi password without them having to ask, or just taking a few moments

to show someone around – these are all simple gestures that convey something much bigger.

3 **Secret Buddies** – Assign everyone on the team a 'Secret Buddy' for the month. Their job is just to keep an eye on that person and make sure they seem happy. You can leave them secret gifts on their desk or send them a virtual postcard from an anonymous email address. Doing this even with a small team creates hundreds of opportunities for the giving, receiving and witnessing of kindness and of course it also becomes a fun game to try and guess who your secret benefactor is (as well as practising your stealth-kindness skills so you don't get found out yourself!).

4 **Kind HR** – Yes, HR can sometimes be in the way of our kind instincts, but HR policies can say a lot about a company's culture. An easy signifier of kindness is to give people the day off on their birthday. Flexible working, whether it's simply 'work from home' guidance or a four-day working week, is another. And how about a duvet day once a quarter, where you can just phone up and say you're knackered and need a day in bed? All of these can be relatively simple to implement and don't cost the business a lot of money. I should know, because my company does all of them.

5 **Being kind to the 'support team'** – As we discussed earlier in Principle 4: 'People First, Work Second. Always.', behind every high-performing colleague is their support team. Find a way to say thank you to partners, friends, housemates, kids or pets for keeping your colleague's spirits high. It could be a big party or a simple card.

6 **Employee volunteering** – Some organizations give their staff two to three days a year to go off and volunteer their time for a charity or community group, while still receiving their full pay. This is such a win-win-win opportunity: the employee feels seen and valued and grateful that they are able to support a cause that is important to them, the organization often benefits from the learning that the employee brings back to their day job and the organization has a presence in the community, often winning kudos, gaining brand awareness and sometimes even winning new business from it.

7 **Charity fundraising or a joint community project** – Raising money for a good cause, or spending a day as a team helping a local community organization or school is a great way to bring people together. Invite colleagues to nominate causes close to their hearts and spend a day spreading kindness together – with everyone working together as humans and equals, away from the trappings of day-to-day hierarchy.

8 **Friday Kudos** – ask everyone to share their 'Wins of the Week' and give kudos to others (this can be at an 'all-hands' meeting, or on email or a Slack channel). Everyone loves to feel valued and what I find when we do this in our own team is that we all learn more about the challenges each other is facing, as well as becoming better informed on what's happening outside of our own work.

KINDNESS HERO: CASE STUDY
JAMES & JOHN TIMPSON – 'WE'RE A PEOPLE BUSINESS.'

One of the kindness heroes of British business is the Timpson Group, a family business run by son James Timpson (CEO) and his father John (chairman and former long-time CEO). Timpson is the UK's leading retail service provider, currently with over 5,000 staff and 2,200 stores. Known primarily as a high-street cobblers and for key-cutting, the business also incorporates the Snappy Snaps photo printing brand, as well as engraving, signs, watch straps, trophies and much more.

John Timpson subscribes to the mantra that kindness is good for business. 'I've discovered that the right way to run a business is through kindness. If you're good to people, then it's good for business,' he said. Timpson runs skills training workshops in prisons and makes a conscious effort to recruit ex-offenders to work for them when they leave. Around 10 per cent of Timpson staff are former prisoners and while this has societal benefits, it's good for business too, driving retention and loyalty among his team.

Timpson puts a lot of trust in its employees: 'We don't do market research, we don't have a marketing department and we don't employ a PR company. The materials we use are a small per cent of the business, but a large slice of the cost of what we do is the people. I've always said that if we have great people, we have a good business.'

Staff are given the day off on their birthday and receive a weekly bonus. They have access to a fleet of holiday properties owned by the firm that can be used free of charge. Timpson has run the 'Dreams Come True' Initiative for his staff for the last few years, which seeks to use company money to do exactly that. So far, the initiative has helped staff to pay for dental treatment, IVF, disabled access in the home, trips abroad to visit long-lost relatives and even a wedding in Las Vegas.

Timpson is a remarkable business. It's not necessarily the first brand you would associate with being a 'people business', but the reality is that people drive the performance of all businesses. And while John Timpson's philosophy and approach may seem unorthodox, it's actually pretty straightforward: to get the most value out of the biggest expenditure line on his P&L – the people – by looking after them, valuing them, trusting them and listening to them. Kindness being at the heart of business is pretty simple when you look at it like that.

This philosophy has been wholeheartedly embraced by his son, James. He told me: 'I'm the most commercial person you will find anywhere. The financial results are the most important thing. Yet, I've just signed off us paying three and half grand (£3,500) for a holiday for a couple who work for us, because they've had a really tough time. And they're getting into American sports and they're gonna have a wonderful time there next year. And so why am I doing that? Number one, I'm doing that as a thank you to them. Number two, I also know that when they come back, they'll work incredibly hard and they won't leave. And they will be an ambassador for our culture too. So, it works both ways.'

To keep the conversation about kindness going, Timpson runs a 'Random Acts of Kindness Award' for staff. Every month, the best five stories from colleagues are rewarded with cash vouchers of £50 and the competition acts as a brilliant way to keep a steady stream of stories circulating around the WhatsApp groups and email accounts of its 5,000-strong team. Timpson is a business built on people and stories – and living proof that a kind working culture gets results.

> 'LEADERSHIP IS LIKE A TEA BAG. YOU DON'T KNOW
> HOW STRONG IT IS UNTIL IT'S IN HOT WATER.'
>
> **Dame Julia Cleverdon DCVO, CBE, British Charity Leader**

Kindness When Times are Tough

A kind culture when times are good feels like a warm fuzzy glow but when times are tough, a kind culture can be the difference between things falling apart versus not. All that time and energy to build kindness and trust, and develop a psychologically safe environment for people to thrive in, really comes into its own when you need to have challenging conversations or make the toughest decisions. And while of course it's true that such moments diminish the trust and psychological safety that people feel (how could they not?), a Kindful culture makes it much easier to get to the other side and start rebuilding everyone's faith and morale. So, let's talk about handling conflicts and mistakes, dealing with bad behaviour and what happens when you need to make cutbacks or have to fire someone or make them redundant.

Kindful Conflict

Conflict is inevitable and it's even more likely to occur when you have a group of motivated and conscientious people who care about the work they're doing than when you have the opposite. There is a kind way to disagree and ways that you can turn this into something healthy rather than something toxic.

HEALTHY TENSION

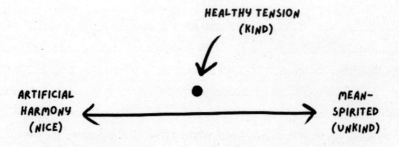

Toxic cultures just let conflict run loose and let the strongest (or most senior) person win. This, of course, is unkind to everyone (even the 'winners' don't learn anything or grow). Nice cultures avoid all conflict and therefore become unproductive. But sometimes conflicts or disagreements are exactly the things that challenge us to see beyond our biases to be better. Handled correctly, conflict is healthy (we just need to make sure we are in the right emotional place to make it kind). Remember, one of the definitions of kindness is 'limiting the damage'. It's up to us to regulate ourselves with this in mind.

Healthy tension requires us to be open-minded enough to recognize that there are things that we don't know and perspectives that even though we might not share, could make us better. This simple graphic illustrates this point. At one end we have the idea of 'artificial harmony', where we choose the 'nice' option and ignore the fact that there is conflict altogether. This may work temporarily, but over time the resentment or bad feeling festers and becomes toxic. At the other end of the scale is conflict that is not kind to the person – unnecessarily vitriolic or mean-spirited. Healthy tension, somewhere in the middle, will ensure a more robust conversation and more productive outcomes.

'I LIKE TO SAY A TEAM IS A GENIUS. AND IT'S ONLY A GENIUS IF PEOPLE ARE BRINGING DIFFERENT EXPERIENCES, PERSPECTIVES AND IDEAS TO THE CONVERSATION. SO DIVERSITY IN THE TEAM IS REALLY IMPORTANT.'

James Reed, Chairman & CEO of The Reed Group

Inviting Dissent

As a leader, my job isn't to drive the loudest consensus, it's to get the best outcome. We need to avoid 'group-think' and ensure that if someone has a better idea, they feel comfortable enough to break ranks. Remember back in Principle Two, we talked about the idea of avoiding self-affirming questions ('does that make sense?', 'we're good, right?', and so on)? Far better to invite dissent and healthy disagreement or challenge, with open-ended questions like 'what are the alternatives?' or 'what still niggles about this decision?', so that you don't allow group-think to shut down the process of making the best decision.

NONVIOLENT COMMUNICATION

Marshall Rosenberg's influential book, *Nonviolent Communication*, is one of the cornerstones of empathetic listening. His idea is that 'Judgments, criticisms, diagnoses, and interpretations of others are all alienated expressions of our needs'.[6] Nonviolent communication helps people to work more collaboratively and kindly to explore both their unmet needs and those of each other, rather than playing out those needs in the midst of unkind conflict. There are two important questions asked by Rosenberg in the book. The first is 'what is alive in you?', or to put it another way, 'what are you feeling?'. The second is 'what would make life more wonderful?' or 'what are the unmet needs you have that I can help to be met?'. While this seems straightforward, it can be incredibly delicate and tricky territory to navigate, especially if emotions run high during a conflict. This is all the more reason that the first strategy for kind conflict is 'avoid them until you're ready'.

'WHAT WAS THE FEELING, WHAT'S THE REQUEST?'

As you bring a conversation where there has been conflict to a hopefully amicable close, there are two questions worth summarizing for each other. The first is 'what was the feeling, for me and for you?' and the second is 'Moving forward, what is the request (or requests)?'. These two simple questions are a way to bring some harmony and respect back into the dynamic and to make sure you're concluding in an amicable way with mutual understanding. If you feel confident that things are ending well, then asking each other to repeat back the other's requests is a great way to increase the level of comfort and mutual understanding.

WHEN YOU SHOULD AVOID CONFLICT

Most of us are eager to shy away from conflict even more than we wish to avoid facing feedback. Conflict can feel genuinely threatening to our Lizard Brains and it is important to navigate potential conflicts with a lot of caution. There is often a narrative around conflict that says 'fronting up' to the people who disagree with us or criticize us is professional and that having a thick skin so that we are not fazed by conflict is preferable. Avoiding conflict can be seen as cowardice, but there are times when it's not cowardly, it's actually the wisest move.

Leadership coach Christina Kisley is often brought in to help deal with the fallout from conflicts that didn't achieve their objective for anyone involved. She says: 'Often times, people get into situations of conflict when they're not really ready. If you know you're walking into a conflict, you have to ask the basic questions, like "can I do this without attacking the person?". And if the answer is no, then you've got to walk away. Before you have that conversation, you need to calm down and process your own shit first. Or we're already in conflict and we just keep going when we really know we shouldn't. It can be hard to call "Time Out!" but that's often exactly what's needed if we want to have genuinely robust and kind conversations.'

HALT!

The acronym HALT can help here: Never engage in conflict, even over email (perhaps *especially* over email!) when you're Hungry, Angry, Lonely or Tired. It takes a certain amount of self-awareness and occasionally if we're mad at someone and want to hit reply, it also takes a huge amount of self-control. But avoiding the conflict in that moment and waiting until we have calmed down is the kindest way to deal with conflict. Doing so limits the damage of your own words on others.

HOW MISTAKES ARE HANDLED

There's a difference between mistakes and negligence. Negligence is where the proper care has not been taken. In cases where negligence puts people or assets at risk, or when behaviour is knowingly wide of the expected standards, then this is clearly a serious issue that needs acting upon. Mistakes, on the other hand, are where someone has taken their best guess, or tried something, and it turned out to be misguided or wrong. Mistakes don't lack care, they just lack the right data or judgement. We all make mistakes, mistakes are part and parcel of work.

There are three ways your organization can deal with mistakes: attach blame to them, ignore them or learn from them. Attaching blame to mistakes is unkind. Making someone feel guilt or shame about something they've probably tried hard to get right only leads to lower morale and a culture of fear. When people are scared to make mistakes, they learn to stop taking guesses, so it slows everything down until there's enough data to make a perfect decision rather than a best guess. It stifles innovation because people are afraid to try new things and it encourages people to see their team as a group of individual missions rather than a collective who have each other's backs.

Mistakes aren't ideal. They're the proof that something could be done better than it was done. And that's an opportunity to get better. When we ignore mistakes, we are telling a bigger story: that average is OK, that we're OK with denying people the opportunities to grow, that we're not as committed to our mission as we say we are. But when we learn from mistakes, we grow. The kind thing to do is to separate the mistake from the person who made it and use the mistake as an opportunity not just for personal growth but for team growth too. Interrogating what went wrong is where we get the best data so that it goes right next time and it allows us to continuously improve.

The best leaders create a safe space to make mistakes. This is the essence of psychological safety. By being kind but rigorous, we get to couch potentially bruising interrogations of mistakes with a warmth and generosity that makes them safe enough to bear. We may even celebrate mistakes, because they show us how often we get it right and remind us that we're human after all. And in doing so, we foster more creativity, a healthier appetite for risk and a mindset that pushes us forward by saying that while we don't need to get everything right, we sure as hell will try our best to.

Dealing with Bad Behaviour

When someone's behaviour is unkind, disruptive, or damaging to the organization's work, it needs to be called out. The 'nice' approach is to ignore it and hope it goes away, but letting bad behaviour slide does everyone else on the team a disservice: they have to suffer the consequences of that person's behaviour, or at the very least, it sends a message that standards don't matter. There are a few simple rules that can help us do this kindly:

- Praise in public, but raise bad behaviour issues in private.
- Discuss the behaviour, not the person ('this thing that happened falls short of what we need' vs 'you've screwed up').
- Make clear the future expectations and boundaries.
- Humanize it (former charity CEO Fiona Dawe told me about a time when she said during a disciplinary procedure: 'You've made me have to act like a grumpy headmistress and I hate having to be *that* person!').
- Remember that in most cases, people are remorseful and embarrassed. Use humour to rebuild trust.
- Dignity always matters.

How to Fire Someone Kindly

Most of the hardest moments in my career have been when I've had to start a meeting, knowing that at the end of that meeting someone will no longer have a job, either due to redundancy or poor performance. I remember one particular case where the person was an absolute star in the organization, but the project had come to an end, there was no budget to keep them on and we had no choice but to let them go. The meeting was nervy and emotional (all three of us in the room cried) and it felt like the worst possible decision for someone who had given their all to the organization for such a long time.

There isn't really a script for these moments, but there are some basic principles. I always try to focus as much of my thinking on the question of 'what would a dignified exit look like for this person?' (remembering to treat people how they want to be treated).

Truth matters. If there's any chance that someone is arriving in a meeting expecting to be fired, then address it directly in the first few sentences. They won't listen to anything else you're trying to sweeten the pill with while that question is still hanging over them.

Grace matters, too. In such moments, our Lizard Brains often make us speed up, perhaps through a wish to be out of the discomfort as soon as possible, but it's important to be led by the person's reaction to the news, not your own agenda. Give them a break, or postpone the discussion until the next day if that's what they need. I usually offer people the choice as to whether to take the rest of the day off, go out for a walk for an hour, or carry on as normal.

Unless there are matters of mistrust, it's important for people to be able to process the decision before they say their goodbyes to colleagues. And one thing that is often appreciated is to ask the person at the end of the meeting, 'How would you like this information to be told to colleagues and is there a set of words that we could all agree to use with clients or other stakeholders?'. Another good question is 'What can we do to support you in this transition?'. They might want to access some CV or interview practice, a glowing reference, or the funds to finish off a qualification they'd started with you. I tend to be open-minded and as financially generous as the situation allows.

These tough moments are where we figure out who we really are. Firing people unkindly, or doing it the cowardly way by text message, or scrimping on decency because someone is halfway out the door might be tempting if you live with a scarcity mindset or believe the 'business bastard' myth and want to seem 'alpha'. But it's astonishingly short-sighted. Suddenly, you have an unsettled team, all wondering if they will be next, and you've sent the signal that you only believe in treating people with kindness when it's easy. Exits are also where you can either choose to honour someone's commitment to you – or have them tell the world, forevermore, that you didn't. Trust and psychological safety are hard-won but easily squandered.

Perpetuating Kindness

This eighth and final principle reminds us that the quiet power of kindness has a life of its own. Our own kind actions are appreciated, but the ripple effects derived from us creating the right culture are exponential. We want to role-model kindness with our own behaviour, but more importantly, it's about how we create the spaces, windows, vessels, excuses and permissions for others to be kind.

Questions for Reflection

- Who are your cultural architects (the people who can instil, reinforce and develop the culture of kindness in your team)?
- Which of the ideas here about a Kindful culture resonate the most with you? What steps can you take to bring them to life for your team?
- What are the best ways to get people in your team talking about and thinking about kindness as often as possible?

Kindness Challenge: Building a Kindful Culture

We have reached our final kindness challenge. I hope that at times we have taken you to the edge of your comfort zone and that you've felt inspired and excited by your Kindfulness practice. For this final challenge, the focus is on helping others to perpetuate kindness. This final challenge mirrors our first one in its simplicity: In line with your authentic self, find ways to start conversations about, or draw attention to, the kindness of others. This could be a Timpson or Pizza Pilgrims-inspired sharing of kindness stories, through bringing them in as a topic in meetings, asking others to nominate their kindness heroes, or anything else that feels like it fits with your leadership style. Notice what happens. This creation is the essence of Kindfulness at Work.

'WITH EVERYTHING THAT'S WRONG WITH THE WORLD, THE TIME FOR KINDNESS IS NOW. SO WHY DON'T WE START NOW?'

LORD JOHN BIRD, FOUNDER OF THE *BIG ISSUE*

Graham Allco

FINAL THOUGHTS

'I HAVE THREE TREASURES THAT I HOLD AND GUARD. THE FIRST IS KINDNESS. THE SECOND IS SIMPLICITY. THE THIRD IS HUMBLENESS. WITH KINDNESS, ONE CAN BE COURAGEOUS. WITH SIMPLICITY, ONE CAN BE GENEROUS. WITH HUMBLENESS, ONE CAN BE THE LEAD TO PROVIDE GUIDANCE.

'NOW, IF ONE ABANDONS KINDNESS AND YET TRIES TO BE COURAGEOUS, IF ONE ABANDONS SIMPLICITY AND TRIES TO BE GENEROUS, IF ONE ABANDONS HUMBLENESS AND TRIES TO LEAD WITH GUIDANCE, HE IS DOOMED TO PERISH.'

Lao Tzu

Just as I was finishing this book, in September 2023, my granny died. She was 97. She was our family's queen – born in the same year as Queen Elizabeth II and living almost exactly a year longer. Elma Vera Allcott was the embodiment of kindness and love throughout her life. After she died, we all went round to her house and each took home something to remember her by. I took a fruit bowl, because I'd remembered a couple of years earlier, she had joked, 'Graham, I'm going to die soon, so I think you should have this.' She was as funny as she was kind.

On her bedside table was a pile of about 20 books and in and among her cricket biographies and travel books were five of mine. While she was alive, I'd had no idea she'd kept all of my books right there by the side of her bed – she was truly my biggest fan.

A few weeks later, my dad cleared out the wardrobe in her spare room. It had a section in it that was a mirror and the mirror doubled up as a cupboard. When he opened the cupboard, he was astonished by what he found there. Piled high, the full length of the mirror, was every single piece of correspondence from her three grandchildren – every letter, postcard, Christmas card, thank-you card, every picture we'd drawn for her at school. Dad spent time sorting them into piles and when we scattered her ashes, he presented each of us with a dusty plastic bag that felt like it was filled with the museum exhibits of our lives.

Most of what I found in that plastic bag were things I'd forgotten I'd sent – drawings from primary school, letters written from the village where I lived whilst volunteering in Uganda, hundreds of little snapshots in time. And of course, the more recent ones are digital photos of me with my son, Roscoe, turned into postcards via apps on my phone – kindness and connection, ever evolving.

It feels fitting that I dedicate this book to my granny. From all those summer holidays staying with her on the south coast to her filling our bellies every Christmas, to her always being there with a listening ear, her passing is such a reminder of how simple and quiet kindness can be. And yet at the same time, how powerful.

You've Come So Far...

Thank you for being on this journey with me. I'm extremely grateful to have had your attention. In Part One of this book, we looked at the science of kindness and how empathy and kindness build trust and psychological safety and the magical results that ensue. In Part Two, we dispelled the myth of the 'business bastard' and the idea that kindness is somehow weak; we discussed how kindness is a verb, not a noun and how the source code for kindness is an abundance mentality. Then, in Part Three, we looked at the Eight Principles of Kindfulness at Work. I hope these have challenged you to think (and act) differently in your own role.

Kindness is a practice, so as we conclude, I want to encourage you to keep practising. But I also want you to remember that kindness starts with you and that just because you keep up the practice, it doesn't mean you will always be perfect. I'll admit that despite being focused on kindness for much of my waking life over the last few years, I regularly screw up or fall short of where I want to be. It's up to all of us to keep practising, with the only comparison question being, 'Am I more Kindful than my former self?'

I always think the magic of books are their ability to connect. I'd love to connect and hear your stories. You can email me at graham@grahamallcott. com. And if you'd like a regular drip-feed of these ideas (and more) in your life, then I have a weekly Sunday email. You can sign up by filling in the form at www .grahamallcott.com. Finally, there are accompanying resources for this book on my site, too, at www.grahamallcott.com/kindful.

You've come so far. We've come so far.

...But Together, We Can Go Further

There are so many people out there doing incredible work to perpetuate kindness, many of whom I've been fortunate enough to meet on this journey. I urge you to check out the annual KindFest[1] online conference, or support Nahla Summers from 'Culture of Kindness' doing her annual 'kindness-raising' challenges and working with organizations, or follow some of the many of the online activists and kindness champions like Time for Kindness or the Random Acts of Kindness Foundation who are helping to make this not just an idea, but a whole movement.

'KINDNESS IS ONE THING, BUT IF YOU'RE WORKING FOR PHILLIP MORRIS AND YOUR WORK IS GIVING CANCER TO TEENAGERS IN THE DEVELOPING WORLD, THEN IT'S TIME TO TAKE OWNERSHIP OF WHAT YOU CREATE.'

Seth Godin, Author, Entrepreneur and Speaker

Where Next for Kindfulness at Work?

This book has been about how to operate with Kindfulness in your work. If we have dismantled some of those scarcity narratives en masse, I truly believe this would be an evolution of capitalism and a quiet revolution in our society. Kindfulness has the power to cause a ripple effect that spreads to all kinds of other ways that we can be better in how we work and live.

Maybe it's because I'm an eternal optimist, or maybe it's because I've spent the last few years immersed in kindness, but I firmly believe the future will be kinder than now. I see a future where the relationship between businesses and their customers will be more firmly rooted in their ethical decision-making. Consumers will increasingly vote with their wallets by demanding kinder working practices and businesses will be left behind if they don't embrace kindness.

Automation and AI will make lots of things easier, but ultimately, humans will still have a need to be creative and make a contribution – and skilled, kind, human navigation of difficult decisions or complex ethical dilemmas will become one of the highest-value aspects of our economy.

On our way there, it's up to us to choose kindness as consumers and be Kindful in our leadership and followership – to join the movements like B Corp, Conscious Capitalism, the Good Business Charter, the 4 Day Week Campaign and many others that call for more systemic kindness in our working world and fight for the big ideas that we know will perpetuate kindness for tomorrow.

But while we have our eyes on the big things, we should never forget that the small things matter, too. This book began life with me walking around Rome, thinking about why kindness was such an emotive topic, so it seems only fitting to end where we began, in some kind of infinitely perpetuating loop of kindness.

One of my favourite examples of kindness comes from Italy. It's an age-old tradition that grew from the coffee shops of Naples: Caffè Sospeso. Caffè Sospeso translates, roughly, as 'a suspended coffee' and the idea is simple. When you buy your morning coffee, you ask for an extra one – a Caffè Sospeso. The owner of the coffee shop takes your money and puts your order ticket in the Caffè Sospeso jar. Anyone in need of a coffee who can't afford one can simply come in, take that ticket and claim the suspended coffee you paid for.

For decades, Italians have been buying Caffè Sospeso for each other. It's a regular, miniature embracing of abundance mentality: that we have enough ourselves and that there's enough for us all if we share.

For me, the beauty in this small act of kindness is the anonymity. It's not 'helping out my friend', or 'being kind so that I get something back later'. No. Much like an Italian espresso, it's the pure, unadulterated form of kindness. Just one human being deciding to help another, with nothing to be gained other than protecting and reinforcing the simple yet powerful idea that lives within all of our minds: that we are richer with kindness than without it. That we are stronger in co-operation than in competition and that while it doesn't need to be complicated, the future of our species depends on us being kinder to each other and to the world around us. And it's a great example of Kindfulness at work – the owner of the coffee shop just found an old jar and wrote the words 'caffè sospeso' on it. They created the vessel for kindness. Being Kindful is as much about creating the conditions and the world where it's easy for others to be kind, as it is being kinder ourselves. That one single action – finding the jar – inspiring a thousand more.

There are so many people who will tell you that kindness has no place at work and some will even tell you it has little place in life. Go tell them to wake up and smell the coffee!

MORE EMPATHY

LESS GREED

MORE RESPECT

ALL I'VE GOT TO SAY HAS
ALREADY BEEN SAID

I MEAN, YOU HEARD IT FROM
YOURSELF
WHEN YOU WERE LYING IN YOUR
BED AND COULDN'T SLEEP
THINKING 'COULDN'T WE BE
DOING THIS
DIFFERENTLY'?

KAE TEMPEST, 'PEOPLE'S FACES'

Graham Allc

THANK YOU

While it's only my name on the cover, books are always a community effort. In addition, so many people's acts of kindness, support and inspiration have over the years inspired my own.

Thank you to my son Roscoe for teaching me more about kindness and what matters than anyone else in this world, and to Chaz for being such a brilliant co-parent through it all. Mum, Dad, Heather, Jo (and not forgetting Granny) – you're all part of a very solid foundation, which I'm really grateful for.

This book has taken a while to crystallize, so thanks to Ian Hallsworth, Allie Collins, Jane Donovan and all at Bloomsbury, Lydia Yadi for helping me birth the idea, my brilliant agent Clare Grist-Taylor, Chris Kisley (I'm so lucky to have you as my Kindful partner-in-crime), my assistant Emilie Stolt for being an incredible support, especially in the moments I was doubting myself – I could not have done this without you.

Many others have helped me develop the ideas, given feedback on individual chapters or helped when something was stuck. Thank you to Ray Sagayam, Ayanna Coleman, Elloa Barbour, Dr Catherine Pitfield, Alison Jones, Grace Marshall, Martin Farrell, David McQueen, Sophie Devonshire, Mark Leruste and Jodie Cook.

Thank you to Kae Tempest for allowing me to use your beautiful lyrics at the end of this book. And Mafalda Casanova – your wonderful illustrations have really helped me bring these ideas to life.

Thanks to everyone at Think Productive, especially Elena Kerrigan and Jess Scott for being constant cheerleaders. And away from work, so many people did their best to keep me sane with support and friendship: Kate McGuire, Elloa and Nick, Danny and Lucy, Esther and Nick, Elise, Nathan, Anthony, Seb, Jeremy, Caroline, Agnes, Derek, Asta, Rob Mac, Chris, Alison, Martha and Pars. And a special thanks to Meg. You're unreal, you are.

A lot of people gave up their time to be part of focus groups. Your feedback and ideas really helped shape this book. Thank you to Rachel Tuxworth, Nicola Talbot, Shona Chambers, Matthew Rayner, Juliet Flynn, Pauline Randles, Ian Adderley, Hannah West, Rumyana Hallingstad, Esther Clarson, Gordon Little, Charlie Hill, Emmeline Hannelly, Helen Holdsworth, Emma Law, Steve Acklam, Teresa Hicks, Laura Woodcock, Rob Cade and Joanna Parry.

This book has a lot of people's voices in it because there isn't one single way to 'do' kindness. The journey of discovery you've all had me on has been inspiring. Thank you to the following people for giving up your time to talk about kindness with me: Julie Brown, Emma Law, Paul Santagata, Nick Jenkins, General Stanley McChrystal, David Bradford, Carole Robin, Fiona Dawe, Jonathan Austin, Laura Woodcock, Greer Rios, Rob Cade, L. David Marquet, Matt Cowdroy, Teresa Hicks, Seth Godin, Sarah Stein Greenberg, Janet Leighton, Cal Newport, Colin Bennett, NK Chaudhary, Michael Norton, Lauren Currie, Sarah Browning, Susie Hills, Julie Nerney, James Timpson, Lisa Smosarski, Carl Honoré, Juliet Flynn, Martin Farrell, Thom Elliot, Professor Robin Banerjee, James Reed, Lord John Bird, Ole Kassow, Denise Nurse, Rachel Forde, Emily Change, Julian Richer, Nahla Summers, Charles Davies, Tom Nixon, Abudu Waiswa Sallam and Sally-Anne Airey.

A book like this makes you think long and hard about your kindness role models over the years. I'm so grateful to people like Max McLoughlin, Elena Kerrigan, Julia Poole, Fiona Dawe, Lizzie Cole, Christopher Spence, Colette Heneghan, Charlene Allcott, Fokke Kooistra, Hayley Watts, Grace Marshall and Lee Cottier for helping me shape my (imperfect) Kindfulness practice over many years.

QUOTED MATERIAL

Booth, David & Hachiya, Masayuki (2004). *The Arts Go to School: Classroom-based Activities that Focus on Music, Painting, Drama, Movement, Media, and More.* (p. 14). Pembroke Publishers Limited.

Brown, Julie. *2020 Kindness & Leadership 50 Leading Lights.* Available at: https://www.kindnessrules.co.uk/our-candidate/2020/

Covey, S.M. & Merrill, R.R. (2006). *The Speed of Trust: The One Thing That Changes Everything.* Simon & Schuster.

Grant, A. (12 February 2021). @adamgrant on Instagram: https://www.instagram.com/p/CLMc8hnpP6z/?igshid=ZWI2YzEzYmMxYg per cent3D per cent3D

Bartlett, Stephen (May 2023): Stephen Bartlett on LinkedIn: https://www.linkedin.com/posts/stevenbartlett-123_the-small-interactions-you-have-with-people-activity-7054755592124399616-g7HG/?utm_source=share&utm_medium=member_desktop

Frank Fonds, Anne (2019). *Anne Frank: The Collected Works.* Bloomsbury Publishing.

Vaynerchuk, G. (9 February 2020). @garyvee on X/Twitter: https://twitter.com/garyvee/status/1226552751800238081

Louden, J. (2005). *Woman's Comfort Book: A Self-Nurturing Guide for Restoring Balance in Your Life.* HarperCollins (p. 2).

Brach, T. (2004). *Radical Acceptance: Embracing Your Life With the Heart of a Buddha.* Bantam (p. 3).

Slezak, Walter (19 June 1956). *Pittsburgh Post-Gazette, Hollywood* by Sheilah Graham, Quote p. 22, col. 4, Pittsburgh, Pennsylvania. (Newspapers.com).

Brown, B. (2018). *Dare to Lead: Brave Work. Tough Conversations. Whole Hearts.* Random House.

Alda, A. (2005). *Never Have Your Dog Stuffed: And Other Things I've Learned.* Random House.

Obama, Michelle (5 September 2012). Michelle Obama's full DNC 2012 speech: https://www.youtube.com/watch?v=47bdOFekU44. Transcript: https://www.ft.com/content/42ee17d8-f6ff-11e1-827f-00144feabdc0

Feloni, R. (29 July 2014). 'Jerry Seinfeld Gives 2 Smart Pieces of Career Advice', *Business Insider*. https://www.businessinsider.com/jerry-seinfeld-ama-career-advice-2014-7?r=US&IR=T.

The Economist (9 February 2019). 'What John Ruskin Can Teach Modern Britain': https://www.economist.com/britain/2019/02/09/what-john-ruskin-can-teach-modern-britain.

Maher, P. & Dorr, M.K. (2009). *Miles on Miles: Interviews and Encounters with Miles Davis*. Chicago Review Press (p. 70).

Ferriss, T. (2007). *The 4-Hour Work Week: Escape 9–5, Live Anywhere, and Join the New Rich*. Crown.

Al Jazeera English (2019). Alain de Botton and Ayishat Akanbi I Studio B: Unscripted. https://www.youtube.com/watch?v=NZU7mumpY4U

Solnit, R. (2017). 'We Could Be Heroes: An Election-Year Letter', *Guardian*, 14 July. https://www.theguardian.com/commentisfree/2012/oct/15/letter-dismal-allies-us-left.

Grayson, D. (6 April 2020). 'Doing Business Ethically in a Time of Coronavirus'. https://www.ibe.org.uk/resource/doing-business-ethically-in-a-time-of-coronavirus.htm

Tzu, L. *Tao Te Ching*.

Tempest, K. (2019). 'People's Faces' (recorded by Kae Tempest). *The Book of Traps and Lessons*. Courtesy of Domino Publishing Company Ltd.

NOTES

Part One

1 Hamilton, D.R. (2021). *The Five Side Effects of Kindness: This Book Will Make You Feel Better, Be Happier & Live Longer*. Hay House, Inc.
2 Kosfeld, M. et al. (2005). 'Oxytocin Increases Trust in Humans', *Nature*, 435(7042), pp. 673–6.
3 Petersson, M. (2002). 'Chapter 22 Cardiovascular Effects of Oxytocin' in *Progress in Brain Research*, pp. 281–8.
4 Alaerts, K., Taillieu, A., Daniels, N. et al. Oxytocin enhances neural approach towards social and non-social stimuli of high personal relevance. *Sci Rep* 11, 23589 (2021).
5 Weng, H.Y. et al. (2013). 'Compassion Training Alters Altruism and Neural Responses to Suffering', *Psychological Science*, 24(7), pp. 1171–80.
6 Alexander, S. & Baraz, J. (2010). 'The Helper's High': https://greatergood.berkeley.edu /article/item/the_helpers_high.
7 Inagaki, T.K. et al. (2016). 'The Neurobiology of Giving Versus Receiving Support', *Psychosomatic Medicine*, 78(4), pp. 443–53.
8 Ashby, F.G., Isen, A.M. & Turken, A.U. (1999). 'A Neuropsychological Theory of Positive Affect and its Influence on Cognition', *Psychol Rev*, 106: 529–50.
9 Trew, J.L. & Alden, L.E. (2015). 'Kindness Reduces Avoidance Goals in Socially Anxious Individuals', *Motivation and Emotion*, 39(6), pp. 892–907.
10 Qualtrics (2018). 'State of Play: UK Employee Engagement Trends 2018'. Available online at: https://success.qualtrics.com/rs/542-FMF-412/images/EX_PULSE_EBOOK _UK_FINAL.pdf
11 McCraty, R. et al. (1998). 'The Impact of a New Emotional Self-management Program on Stress, Emotions, Heart Rate Variability, DHEA and Cortisol', *Integrative Physiological and Behavioral Science*, 33(2), pp. 151–70.
12 Hamilton, D.R. (2021). *The Five Side Effects of Kindness: This Book Will Make You Feel Better, Be Happier & Live Longer*. Hay House, Inc.
13 Luks, A. (1988). 'Helper's High: Volunteering Makes People Feel Good, Physically and Emotionally. And Like "Runner's Calm", It's Probably Good for Your Health', *Psychology Today*, 22(10), pp. 34–42.
14 Mental Health Foundation (2020). *Kindness and Mental Health*: https://www.mental-health.org.uk/explore-mental-health/kindness.
15 Pressman, S.D., Kraft, T. & Cross, M.P. (2014). 'It's Good to Do Good and Receive Good: The Impact of a "Pay It Forward" Style Kindness Intervention on Giver and Receiver Well-being', *The Journal of Positive Psychology*, 10(4), pp. 293–302.

16 Chancellor, J. et al. (2018). 'Everyday Prosociality in the Workplace: The Reinforcing Benefits of Giving, Getting, and Glimpsing', *Emotion*, 18(4), pp. 507–17.

17 Silvers, J.A. & Haidt, J. (2008). 'Moral Elevation can Induce Nursing', *Emotion*, 8(2), pp. 291–5.

18 McClelland, D.C. & Kirshnit, C. (1988). 'The Effect of Motivational Arousal Through Films on Salivary Immunoglobulin A', *Psychology & Health*, 2(1), pp. 31–52.

19 Seppälä, E., Hutcherson, C.A., Nguyen, D.T.H., Doty, J.R. & Gross, J.J. (2014). 'Loving-kindness Meditation: A Tool to Improve Healthcare Provider Compassion, Resilience, and Patient Care', *Journal of Compassionate Health Care*, 1(1).

20 'Strangers Swap Kidneys in "Pay It Forward" Chain', NBC News, 11 March 2009. https://www.nbcnews.com/health/health-news/strangers-swap-kidneys-pay-it-forward-chain-flna1c9454555

21 Fowler, J.H. & Christakis, N.A. (2010). 'Cooperative Behavior Cascades in Human Social Networks', Proceedings of the National Academy of Sciences of the United States of America, 107(12), 5334–38.

22 'Business Case for Kindness' (2016). U.S. Chamber of Commerce Foundation. Available at: https://www.uschamberfoundation.org/business-kindness/business-case-kindness/survey-results

23 Van Berkhout, E.T. & Malouff, J.M. (2016). 'The Efficacy of Empathy Training: A Meta-analysis of Randomized Controlled Trials', *Journal of Counseling Psychology*, 63(1), pp. 32–41.

24 Delizonna, L. (4 April 2023). 'High-Performing Teams Need Psychological Safety: Here's How to Create It', *Harvard Business Review*: https://hbr.org/2017/08/high-performing-teams-need-psychological-safety-heres-how-to-create-it

25 Seppälä, E. (10 February 2017). 'Why Compassion Is a Better Managerial Tactic than Toughness', *Harvard Business Review*: https://hbr.org/2015/05/why-compassion-is-a-better-managerial-tactic-than-toughness

26 Vianello, Michelangelo, Galliani, Elisa Maria & Haidt, Jonathan (2010). 'Elevation at Work: The Effects of Leaders' Moral Excellence', *The Journal of Positive Psychology*, 5:5, 390–411.

27 Carucci, R. (19 January 2016). 'A 10-Year Study Reveals What Great Executives Know and Do', *Harvard Business Review*: https://hbr.org/2016/01/a-10-year-study-reveals-what-great-executives-know-and-do

28 Edmondson, A.C. & Lei, Z. (2014). 'Psychological Safety: The History, Renaissance, and Future of an Interpersonal Construct', *Annual Review of Organizational Psychology and Organizational Behavior*, 1(1), 23–43.

29 Edmondson, Amy C. 'Psychological Safety': https://amycedmondson.com/psychological-safety

30 Tahir, S. (2021). 'Psychological Safety. CQ Net – Management Skills for Everyone!': https://www.ckju.net/en/dossier/psychological-safety-what-it-why-it-matters-and-how-improve-it

31 Google re: Work – ガイド:「効果的なチームとは何か」を知る. https://rework.withgoogle.com/jp/guides/understanding-team-effectiveness#identify-dynamics-of-effective-teams

32 Sgroi, D. (2015). 'Happiness and Productivity: Understanding the Happy-Productive Worker – Social Market Foundation', *Social Market Foundation*, 27 October. https://www.smf.co.uk/publications/happiness-and-productivity-understanding-the-happy-productive-worker/

33 Anjum, A., Xu, M., Siddiqi, A.F. & Rasool, S.F. (2018). 'An Empirical Study Analyzing Job Productivity in Toxic Workplace Environments', *International Journal of Environmental Research and Public Health*, 15(5), 1035.

34 SHRM (2023) '2022 Workplace Learning & Development Trends,' *SHRM, 21 December*. *https://www.shrm.org/topics-tools/research/2022-workplace-learning-development -trends*.

35 Porath, C. and Pearson, C. (2019). 'The Price of Incivility', *Harvard Business Review*. https://hbr.org/2013/01/the-price-of-incivilit

36 Dowden, C. (2015). 'Civility Matters! An Evidence-based Review on How to Cultivate a Respectful Federal Public Service', Association of Professional Executives of the Public Service of Canada (APEX). https://apex.gc.ca/wp-content/uploads/2021/04/civility -report-eng.pdf

37 Chancellor, J. et al. (2018). 'Everyday Prosociality in the Workplace: The Reinforcing Benefits of Giving, Getting, and Glimpsing', *Emotion*, 18(4), pp. 507–17.

38 Wang, Y., Zhao, C., Zhang, S., Li, Q., Tian, J., Yang, M., Guo, H., Jia, Y., Zhou, S., Wang, M. & Cao, D. (2022). 'Proactive Personality and Critical Thinking in Chinese Medical Students: The Moderating Effects of Psychological Safety and Academic Self-efficacy', *Frontiers in Psychology*, 13.

39 Kaushik, A. (2007). *Web Analytics: An Hour a Day*, Sybex.

40 Sturt, D. & Nordstrom, T. (18 September 2014). 'How to Meet the One Person Who Could Change Your Life', Forbes. https://www.forbes.com/sites/davidsturt /2014/09/18/how-to-meet-the-one-person-who-could-change-your-life/?sh =11eed1641157

41 Gallup, Inc. (1 December 2023). 'How to Improve Employee Engagement in the Workplace' – Gallup. Gallup.com. https://www.gallup.com/workplace/285674/impr ove-employee-engagement-workplace.aspx

42 Higginbottom, K. (11 September 2014). 'Workplace Stress Leads to Less Productive Employees', Forbes. https://www.forbes.com/sites/karenhigginbottom/2014/09/11/ workplace-stress-leads-to-less-productive-employees/?sh=5e47397e31d1

43 Harter, B. & Mann, A. (8 December 2023). 'The Worldwide Employee Engagement Crisis', Gallup.com. https://www.gallup.com/workplace/236495/worldwide-employee -engagement-crisis.aspx?g_source=EMPLOYEE_ENGAGEMENT&g_medium=topic&g _campaign=tiles

44 Rhoades, L., & Eisenberger, R. (2002). 'Perceived organizational support: A review of the literature', *Journal of Applied Psychology*, 87(4), 698–714. https://doi.org/10 .1037/0021-9010.87.4.698

45 https://www.sussex.ac.uk/research/centres/kindness/research/thekindnesstest

46 Rowland, L. & Scott Curry, O. (2019). 'A Range of Kindness Activities Boost Happiness', *The Journal of Social Psychology*, 159:3,pp. 340–3.

47 Seppälä, E. (8 May 2017). 'Proof that Positive Work Cultures are More Productive', *Harvard Business Review*: https://hbr.org/2015/12/proof-that-positive-work-cultures -are-more-productive

48 Robison, B.J. (21 February 2023). 'How the Ritz-Carlton Manages the Mystique', Gallup.com. https://news.gallup.com/businessjournal/112906/how-ritzcarlton-man-ages-mystique.aspx

49 McGonagle, E. (2 June 2021). 'Burger King Promotes Independent Competitors as Covid-19 Restrictions Tighten', *Campaign*. https://www.campaignlive.co.uk/article/burger -king-promotes-independent-competitors-covid-19-restrictions-tighten/1702862

50 Burger King UK (15 December 2020). 'They need you more than ever!', *Twitter*. https://twitter.com/BurgerKingUK/status/1338583450878668801
51 Tarlton, A. (11 July 2022). '50 Brands Giving Back to the Community During the COVID-19 Pandemic', *USA Today*. https://eu.usatoday.com/story/tech/reviewedcom/2020 /07/16/50-brands-giving-back-community-during-covid-19-pandemic/5449545002/
52 Porath, C. and Pearson, C. (2019). 'The Price of Incivility', *Harvard Business Review*. https://hbr.org/2013/01/the-price-of-incivility.

Part Two

1 ABC News (16 March 2019). 'The Dropout Part 3: Former Theranos Employees Claim Toxic Work Culture' [Video]. YouTube. https://www.youtube.com/watch?v=bpBELR366c4
2 BBC News (4 January 2022). 'Elizabeth Holmes: Theranos Founder Convicted of Fraud': https://www.bbc.co.uk/news/world-us-canada-59734254
3 Waikar, S. (2018). 'What Can We Learn from the Downfall of Theranos?', Stanford Graduate School of Business: https://www.gsb.stanford.edu/insights/what-can-we -learn-downfall-theranos.
4 Bannatyne, D. (2007). *Anyone Can Do It*. London: Orion.
5 Durot, M. (15 June 2022). 'Warren Buffett Has Now Given Record $48 Billion to Charity', *Forbes*. https://www.forbes.com/sites/mattdurot/2022/06/14/warren-buf-fett-just-gave-another-4-billion-to-charity/
6 Zenger, J. and Folkman, J. (2014). *I'm the Boss! Why Should I Care If You Like Me?* https://hbr.org/2013/05/im-the-boss-why-should-i-care.
7 Smith, A. (2008). *An Inquiry into the Nature and Causes of the Wealth of Nations: A Selected Edition*, Oxford Paperbacks.
8 Smith, A. (2006). *The Theory of Moral Sentiments*, Mineola, N.Y.: Dover Publications.
9 BBC News (19 August 2014). 'Former Microsoft Boss Steve Ballmer Leaves Firm': https://www.bbc.co.uk/news/business-28861010
10 Literary Hub (16 January 2020). 'The Art of War is Actually a Manual on How to Avoid It' https://lithub.com/the-art-of-war-is-actually-a-manual-on-how-to-avoid-it/
11 Bregman, R. (2021). *Humankind: A Hopeful History*. London: Bloomsbury Publishing.
12 Campbell, A. (11 April 2020). 'Jacinda Ardern's Coronavirus Plan is Working Because, Unlike Others, She's Behaving Like a True Leader', *Independent*.
13 Blackwell, G. (1 June 2020). Jacinda Ardern: 'Political Leaders Can Be Both Empathetic and Strong', *Guardian*.

Part Three: Chapter 1

1 De Botton, A. (2005). *Status Anxiety*. Penguin UK.
2 Donnelly, G.E., Zheng, T., Haisley, E. & Norton, M.I. (2018). 'The Amount and Source of Millionaires' Wealth (Moderately) Predicts Their Happiness', *Personality and Social Psychology Bulletin*, 44(5), 68499. https://doi.org/10.1177/0146167217744766
3 Wignall, N. (10 January 2022). '10 Types of Negative Self-Talk (and How to Correct Them)' https://nickwignall.com/negative-self-talk/#types
4 Brown, B. (2018). *Dare to Lead: Brave Work. Tough Conversations. Whole Hearts.* Random House.

Chapter 2

1 Harnish, V. (2002). *Mastering the Rockerfeller Habits: What You Must Do to Increase the Value of Your Growing Firm.* Gazelles Incorporated.
2 Hsieh, T. (2012). *Delivering Happiness: A Path to Profits, Passion, and Purpose.* New York: BusinessPlus.
3 Marquet, L.D. (2020). *Leadership is Language: The Hidden Power of What You Say and What You Don't.* Portfolio.
4 Godin, S. (2020). *The Practice: Shipping Creative Work.* London: Penguin Business.
5 Greenberg, S. S., & DSchool, S. (2021). *Creative acts for curious people: How to Think, Create, and Lead in Unconventional Ways.* Penguin UK.

Chapter 3

1 Kline, N. (1999). *Time to Think: Listening to Ignite the Human Mind.* Hachette UK.
2 Rogers, C.R. and Farson, R.E. (2021). *Active Listening.* Mockingbird Press.
3 Moyers, Bill. *A World of Ideas* (1989); Drucker, Peter. *Father of Modern Management* IBillMoyers.com. https://billmoyers.com/content/peter-drucker

Chapter 4

1 https://www.independent.co.uk/space/elon-musk-hates-tesla-solarcity-court-b1883151.html
2 Chang, E. (2021). *The Spare Room: Define Your Social Legacy to Live a More Intentional Life and Lead with Authentic Purpose.* Post Hill Press.

Chapter 5

1 LaBouff, J.P., Rowatt, W.C., Johnson, M.K., Tsang, J. & Willerton, G.M. (2012). 'Humble Persons are More Helpful Than Less Humble Persons: Evidence From Three Studies', *The Journal of Positive Psychology*, 7(1), 16–29.
2 Hamley, C. & McClendon, D. (August 1975). 'Linebacking in the LSU 5-4-2 and 4-3-2', *Scholastic Coach*, Column 2, Volume 45, *School Division of Scholastic Magazines*, New York (p. 23).
3 Nunez, K. (9 June 2020). '5 Benefits of Metta Meditation and How to Do It', Healthline. https://www.healthline.com/health/metta-meditation#benefits

Chapter 6

1 Ingall, A. (2022, March 9). Two thirds of people who took part in The Kindness Test think the pandemic has made people kinder. The University of Sussex. https://www.sussex.ac.uk/broadcast/read/57570

2 Epilepsy terminology|Epilepsy Society (11 June 2021). https://epilepsysociety.org.uk/about-epilepsy/epileptic-seizures/epilepsy-terminology
3 Greylock (2015). 'Blitzscaling 18: Brian Chesky on Launching Airbnb and the Challenges of Scale'. https://www.youtube.com/watch?v=W608u6sBFpo.

Chapter 7

1 Two-thirds of people who took part in The Kindness Test think the pandemic has made people kinder. (2022, March 9). BBC Media Centre. https://www.bbc.co.uk/mediacentre/2022/the-kindness-test-results
2 Honoré, C. (2010). *In Praise of Slow: How a Worldwide Movement is Challenging the Cult of Speed*. Hachette UK.
3 Honoré, C. (July, 2005). *In Praise of Slowness*. TED Talks. https://www.ted.com/talks/carl_honore_in_praise_of_slowness?language=en
4 Peters, T. J., & Waterman, R. H. (2004). *In Search of Excellence: Lessons from America's Best-run Companies*. Profile Books(GB)
5 Richer, J. (2019). *The Ethical Capitalist: How to Make Business Work Better for Society*. National Geographic Books
6 Richer, J. (2020). *The Richer Way: How to Get the Best Out of People*. National Geographic Books.

Chapter 8

1 https://raeng.org.uk/policy-and-resources/diversity-and-inclusion-research-and-resources/inclusive-cultures
2 https://gothamculture.com/what-is-organizational-culture-definition/
3 BBC Two – Science & Nature – *Horizon*, 'The England Patient', transcript (23 May 2002). https://www.bbc.co.uk/science/horizon/2001/englandpatienttrans.shtml
4 Frankel, L. P. (2014). *Nice girls don't get the corner office: Unconscious Mistakes Women Make That Sabotage Their Careers*. Business Plus.
5 BBC Radio 4 – *The Anatomy of Kindness* (2022, March 30). BBC. https://www.bbc.co.uk/programmes/m00154cp/episodes/player
6 Rosenberg, M.B. (2015). *Nonviolent Communication: A Language of Life*. Puddle Dancer Press.

Final Thoughts

1 https://www.teamkind.org.uk/

INDEX